Le Corbusier's MAISON CURUTCHET

Alejandro Lapunzina

Le Corbusier's
MAISON CURUTCHET

New York • Princeton Architectural Press

Published by
Princeton Architectural Press
37 East 7th Street
New York, New York 10003
ISBN 1-56898-095-7

© 1997 Alejandro Lapunzina
All rights reserved

No part of this book may be used or reproduced in any
manner without written permission from the publisher
except in the context of reviews.

01 00 99 98 97   5 4 3 2 1
Printed and bound by Data Reproductions Corporation, Rochester Hills, MI

Cover photo: Maison Curutchet, exterior. *Alejandro Lapunzina*
Project editor: Therese Kelly

*Special thanks to Caroline Green, Clare Jacobson,
Mark Lamster, Annie Nitschke, and Sara Stemen
of Princeton Architectural Press*—Kevin C. Lippert, Publisher

Library of Congress Cataloging-in-Publication Data
Lapunzina, Alejandro, 1960-
    Le Corbusier's Maison Curutchet / Alejandro Lapunzina.
    p.   cm.
    Includes bibliographical references
    ISBN 1-56898-095-7 (alk. paper)
    1. Maison Curutchet (La Plata, Argentina) 2. Le Corbusier, 1887-1965
—Criticism and interpretation. 3. Curutchet, Pedro D.—Homes and haunts
—Argentina—La Plata. 4. La Plata (Argentina)—Buildings, structures, etc.
I. Title.
NA7294.L34L36 1997
72'.37'098212—dc21   97-4043
                                                                                              CIP

For a free catalog of other books by Princeton Architectural Press,
call 1.800.722.6657 or visit our web site at www.papress.com.

CONTENTS

4	Acknowledgments
17	Introduction
33	CHAPTER I The Commission
51	CHAPTER II The Design Process
85	CHAPTER III Building Maison Curutchet
123	CHAPTER IV Insertion into Le Corbusier's Oeuvre
151	CHAPTER V The *Promenade Architecturale*, The Eye and the Poetry of Architecture
175	Sources of Illustrations
176	Bibliography

This book dedicated to a thorough study of Maison Curutchet—the result of approximately eight years of work—could not have been possible without the support of several institutions and the assistance of numerous individuals.

I am deeply indebted to the National Endowment for the Humanities Travel Program, and to the Research Board of the University of Illinois at Urbana-Champaign for their grant programs which helped finance archival research at La Fondation Le Corbusier, and the development of other aspects of this project. The Research Board also provided the financial assistance necessary for the publication phase. Similarly I am thankful to La Fondation Le Corbusier in Paris, and to the Francis Loeb Library at Harvard University for allowing me to access their collections. I am especially grateful to Mme Evelyn Trehin, director, and Mme Holy Raveldarisoa, head librarian, of La Fondation Le Corbusier, and to Mary Daniels from the Francis Loeb Library Special Collections for their valuable assistance and good will during the time I spent at both institutions. These two institutions also provided a large number of the illustrations that support and accompany the text.

I am especially indebted to Professor William Curtis, in whose course "Le Corbusier: Ideas and Forms" offered in the 1987 spring semester at Washington University in Saint Louis, the idea of writing about Maison Curutchet emerged. Professor Curtis' comments on the paper that I presented in that course were fundamental not only for the continuation of the project with the objective of writing this book, but also for the development of much of the text. I am also very grateful to Professor Jorge Silvetti of Harvard University Graduate School of Design for allowing me to reproduce the numerous slides that he had taken long ago at Maison Curutchet, and above all, for his willingness to share information and discuss this project with me in the summer of 1990.

I am thankful to Ms. Alcira Curutchet de Goggi for responding to my letters and telephone calls requesting information and facts about her father, Dr. Pedro Curutchet, and the history of the building. Similarly I am grateful to Roger Aujame for the long conversation we had concerning his experiences during the design of Maison Curutchet and to Jerzy Soltan, Professor Emeritus of Harvard University, for sharing information and anecdotes from his experience at the Atelier Le Corbusier in the forties. I am also indebted to Luis and Julio Grossman, the architects responsible for restoring the house, who provided copies of the drawings and photographs, as well as valuable information on the building. Similarly, I am indebted to Claudio Williams (son of Amancio Williams), Nestor Julio Otero, and Cristina Vitalone for their assistance in providing important photographs included in this book.

I am very grateful to my editor, Therese Kelly, for her terrific work with a difficult manuscript. Her questions, advice, challenging criticism, and precise comments were fundamental in clarifying and improving many aspects discussed in this book. I am also thankful to Allison Saltzman and publisher Kevin Lippert of Princeton Architectural Press for believing in this project already in 1993, long before the manuscript was completed.

I am also thankful to my family, especially my mother and my brother, for their logistical support, assistance and encouragement from Argentina; without their help in obtaining and sending me information and materials I could not have developed important parts of this work. I am also grateful to many of my friends and colleagues for their assistance and continuous support. At the risk of forgetting some names, I thank R. Alan Forrester, Hub White, Botond Bognar, Gerardo Caballero, Robert Dermody, Paul Guzzardo, Lorens Holm, Marie-Annick Matovic, José Piñol, Henry Plummer, Christopher Quinn, John Reese, and Robert and Saundra Weddle. Special thanks to Nora Laos, who read the first full version of the manuscript and provided challenging questions and criticism at a critical point in the project.

Finally, I am extremely grateful to my wife Magalí for her support, encouragement, criticism, understanding, and—above all—patience during the long years in which I worked on this project. It is to her and to our two daughters, Andrea and Alejandra, that I dedicate this book.

PLATES

I	Maison Curutchet from the boulevard in summer.
II	Maison Curutchet, exterior.
III	"The Three Melodies." Conceptual diagram of Maison Curutchet's elevation.
IV	Detailed study for the clinic volume.
V	View of the ramp from its intermediate landing.
VI	View of the ramp through the hanging garden.
VII	Detail of residence facade: pan-de-verre, brise soleil, tree.
VIII	View of the park from the terrace-garden.

Maison Curutchet
La Plata, Argentina

II

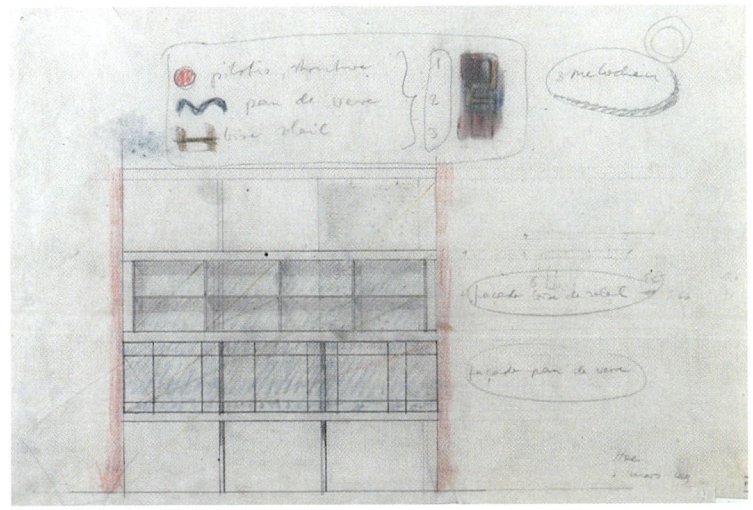

III

IV

v

VI

VII

VIII

Maison Curutchet

INTRODUCTION

The Maison Curutchet, located in La Plata, Argentina, is one of the most significant buildings designed by Le Corbusier, not only for the drama and poetry of its design, but also for the unique story behind its conception and evolution. A combination single-family dwelling and professional medical office, the house was commissioned in 1948 by Dr. Pedro Domingo Curutchet, a well-known, progressive and revolutionary surgeon. He was the quintessential "modern" individual, and thus the ideal Corbusian client. The building's complex program was resolved by Le Corbusier during a relatively short design process with extraordinary intelligence and plasticity, to become one of his most interesting houses. However, despite its unique architectural characteristics and evolution, Maison Curutchet has escaped international renown, remaining one of the least known works in Le Corbusier's oeuvre.

Construction of the house began in 1951 under the supervision of Amancio Williams, one of the most prominent modern Argentinean architects, who was recommended by Le Corbusier; it was completed in the mid-fifties after a long and often conflictive process, having endured numerous technological problems and changes of construction supervisor. The Curutchet family occupied the house for only a short time and virtually abandoned it soon after the first decade of completion, although Dr. Curutchet continued to use the building occasionally as overnight accommodation during his professional trips to La Plata. Little used and poorly maintained for several years, the house fell into disrepair.

However, in 1986-88, in connection with the worldwide celebrations of Le Corbusier's birth centennial, the building was fully restored and proclaimed a national monument by Argentina's commission on national landmarks.[1] The Maison Curutchet is still owned by Dr. Curutchet's family (he died in 1992) and it currently houses La Plata's Colegio de Arquitectos, a professional association of architects from the Province of Buenos Aires.

Le Corbusier designed Maison Curutchet in the 1940s, a period marked by his reevaluation of the architectural postulates he had proposed more than twenty years earlier in *Vers une Architecture*. Thus, it is emblematic of what William Curtis has characterized as Le Corbusier's "period of reassessment" of architectural principles and timeless values, and a reemerging obsession with the harmony of nature.[2] Maison Curutchet is Le Corbusier's first house that achieved completion after World War II, and it is undoubtedly one of the most significant single-family dwellings in the period of transition that followed the war, that is, between the heroic villas of the twenties and the more monumental Villa Shodhan, in Ahmedabad (1956). Maison Curutchet is therefore highly emblematic of this transitional, reflective period of blending old and new architectural postulates.

Furthermore, as several authors have already indicated, it was typical of Le Corbusier to use individual commissions to test and demonstrate his general theory of urbanism.[3] Expectedly, Maison Curutchet did not constitute an exception. Therefore, at the scale of the single-family dwelling, Maison Curutchet also emerges as an emblem of Le Corbusier's urban proposals, especially his project La Ville Radieuse (1930). The differentiation of vehicular and pedestrian circulation, the separation of traffic from living areas, the intertwining of the building with nature, and the clear definition of functional areas (working, living, sleeping, leisure) stand out in Maison Curutchet as clear examples of Le Corbusier's urban principles applied at the scale of the single-family house.

However, aside from its position within Le Corbusier's oeuvre, the Maison Curutchet is a significant work of architecture in its own right. The drama of Maison Curutchet's *promenade architecturale*, the sheer poetic power of its masses and voids, the magnificent ramp, pilotis, brise-soleils, and hanging garden, and the didactic nature of the building's resolution are comparable to the architect's best-known masterpieces. It is one of the most beautiful, spatially dramatic and poetic houses designed by Le Corbusier.

Nevertheless, in spite of the magnificence of its architecture and its significance as a landmark in Le Corbusier's domestic work, Maison Curutchet has remained, curiously, one of the least-known buildings Le Corbusier designed. There has been no thorough analysis of this building, nor has its significance as representative of an important period of Le Corbusier's work been adequately noted. This lacuna in the scholarship of Le Corbusier's architectural production may be attributed to various factors. One is that the design of this

INTRODUCTION

house was contemporaneous with the construction and continued design of the Unité d'Habitation in Marseilles, one of Le Corbusier's most significant buildings. Other reasons may be the small size of the house (compared to Le Corbusier's other, much larger projects undertaken after World War II), and its geographical location, in the rather small city of La Plata, Argentina, far away from the production centers of architectural publications. Furthermore, only the project of the building, that is, the drawings and photographs of the model, was initially included in the well-known publication of Le Corbusier's *Oeuvre Complète*, which may be attributed to Le Corbusier's lack of participation in the actual construction of the building. It was only in compiling the eight volumes of the *Oeuvre Complète* into one single volume that a few photographs of the built house were finally included.[4]

It does not seem unusual then that, despite its architectural value, this small building—located far away from the centers of production of architectural literature, overshadowed by the Unité's symbolism and importance within the architect's oeuvre, and for a long time somehow neglected in its built form by the architect himself—has received little attention from architectural critics and historians. Maison Curutchet has remained buried in the historiography of Le Corbusier's work as just one more "Le Corbusier building" (some have even thought it was just another in the long list of his unrealized projects).[5] However, in recent years, following Le Corbusier's birth centennial and the building's renovation and proclamation as a national monument, Maison Curutchet was "rediscovered." Photographs of the building, most of them accompanied by short articles, were published in numerous European and American architectural journals;[6] yet, all these publications are brief and mostly descriptive, and some even include erroneous and contradictory information.

The purpose of this book is then to present a thorough historical as well as critical study of the building, assessing its significance within Le Corbusier's oeuvre, and its importance as a work of architecture in its own right, with the hope of rescuing it from the long years of undeserved seclusion. In some aspects, Maison Curutchet presents characteristics unique to Le Corbusier's "typical" work (its commission, program, renewed architectural vocabulary, for example) and will be highlighted here. For the most part, though, Maison Curutchet is representative of Le Corbusier's architectural ideas and of his methodology, serving as a model from which to study several aspects of the architect's work: his relationship with clients and collaborators; his design process; the organization, conception and generation of his buildings; and, above all, the poetic dimension of his architecture.

However comprehensive, this study does not pretend to be the ultimate work on the Maison Curutchet. Rather, it attempts to honor it and the visionaries who made it possible. As time slips by, these people, living testimonies of this great building, are slowly disappearing. Le Corbusier died in 1965; Dr. Pedro Curutchet, in 1992; and Amancio Williams, in 1989. Let this work then be an homage to these three great visionary individuals of the twentieth century. Let it also be an homage to all those who had a role in this building: Le Corbusier's collaborators, Bernard Hoesli (who died in the late 1980s) and Roger Aujame (who lives in Meudon, near Paris), Williams' "Curutchet team," the anonymous professionals, carpenters and masons who built it, and all those involved in the restoration and preservation of the building.

Finally, Maison Curutchet is the only built house of the many that Le Corbusier designed for sites on the American continent. Along with the Carpenter Center (located at Harvard University in Cambridge, Massachusetts, and designed and built in the 1960s) it is one of the only two buildings in the Americas exclusively designed by Le Corbusier[7]—and it is the only realized project of the many he developed for sites in Argentina. After having visited the country in 1929, he had hoped to materialize there some of his grandiose ideas on architecture and urban planning. In fact, he had avowedly intended to use Maison Curutchet as a demonstration of his architectural and urban ideas, with the hope of persuading the Argentine government to implement his planning proposal for Buenos Aires. Thus, before continuing with the study of Maison Curutchet, it is necessary to consider the long and mostly unfruitful relationship between Le Corbusier and Argentina.

Le Corbusier and Argentina: 1928-1961
The relationship between Le Corbusier and South America began in the mid-twenties, when the Brazilian coffee magnate, Paulo Prado and the French poet, Blaise Cendrars, encouraged Le Corbusier to visit Brazil through maps and photographs.[8] In those same years, Alejo González Garaño, an Argentinean connoisseur whom Le Corbusier had met in Paris at the home of the duchess of Dato, urged him to visit Buenos Aires. A few years later, in 1929, Amigos del Arte, a group of young intellectuals and artists who were trying to

INTRODUCTION

develop Buenos Aires into an important center of culture, invited Le Corbusier to deliver a series of lectures in Buenos Aires. Amigos del Arte was particularly interested in attracting the avant-garde personalities of the time. Exhibitions, lectures, films and music sessions constituted the core of the activities they organized.[9] The contact with Le Corbusier had been established by Victoria Ocampo, a young and progressive writer and one of the founding members of Amigos del Arte, who had met Le Corbusier in Paris and had already commissioned him a project.

Le Corbusier left Paris aboard the *Giulio Cesare* on September 18, 1929, and arrived in Buenos Aires on October 1.[10] He immediately captured the essence of Buenos Aires' landscape, a city trapped between two endless horizons: the flat countryside known as the *pampas*, and the wide Río de la Plata. Le Corbusier would later write:

> The sky of Argentina? Yes, the only great consolation. For I have seen it, this sky, on the endless plain of grasslands punctuated occasionally by a few weeping willows; it is unlimited, as sparkling by day as by night with a transparent blue light or with myriads of stars; it spreads to all four horizons; to tell the truth, all this landscape is one single and same straight line: the horizon.[11]

Two days after his arrival, Le Corbusier delivered his first lecture, entitled "To free oneself entirely of academic thinking," at the headquarters of Amigos del Arte. In Buenos Aires, he delivered a total of ten lectures, all of which focused on the central themes that Le Corbusier considered relevant to the realm of architecture, from large-scale urbanism and town planning to furniture design. On his way back to Europe, Le Corbusier stopped in Montevideo and Rio de Janeiro where he also lectured. The outcome of this first trip to South America was a book entitled *Précisions sur un état présent de l'architecture et de l'urbanisme*, in which he elaborated on the lectures he had delivered in Argentina, Uruguay and Brazil.[12]

During Le Corbusier's extended stay in Argentina, he had the opportunity to visit many cities and towns near Buenos Aires, such as Avellaneda, Mar del Plata, and La Plata. In Buenos Aires he had also participated in the inaugural flight of the Companía Sudamericana de Aviación, where he met and probably flew with Antoine de Saint-Exupéry.[13] As Argentinean architect and writer Ernesto Katzenstein pointed out, "his diagnoses respecting the city [of Buenos Aires] and its architecture were definite and pessimistic."[14] Neverthe-

MAISON CURUTCHET

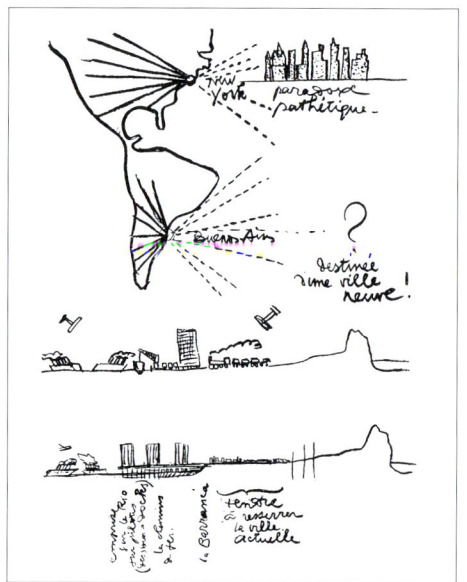

FIG. 1. America, New York, Buenos Aires. One of the drawings Le Corbusier made during his lecture tour in Buenos Aires.

FIG 2. Le Corbusier's vision of Buenos Aires from the Río de la Plata.

INTRODUCTION

less, he had hopes of obtaining commissions from his Argentinean friends, particularly in the realm of urban planning, which in turn could lead to architecture commissions.

The lecture tour was not the first time Le Corbusier had come in contact with Argentine "high culture." In 1928, the writer Victoria Ocampo had asked Le Corbusier to design a house for her in Buenos Aires. The story is well known: Le Corbusier made quick adaptations to his recent and unrealized project for the Villa Meyer, and sent it to Madame Ocampo. Curiously, the writer had simultaneously asked Alejandro Bustillo, a local and well-known eclectic architect, to design a house with a similar program but on a different site. Madame Ocampo decided to build Bustillo's project rather than Le Corbusier's, probably because, as Katzenstein noted, "she needed an experienced professional more than a difficult artist or a polemic youth to carry out her (modern) ideas."[15] However, the relationship between the architect and the writer did not end with this project. On the contrary, during Le Corbusier's trip to Argentina one year later, Madame Ocampo was one of his most conspicuous hosts, and again asked him, however informally, to make several proposals for various sites. As was typical of Le Corbusier, he took the offer far more seriously and bombarded Ocampo with ideas and projects. The best-known among them is a complex of weekend houses just outside of Buenos Aires in Delta del Tigre, which consisted of seventeen clones of the Villa Savoye where, in Le Corbusier's own words, the inhabitants' domestic life "would be set in a Virgilian dream."[16]

Not one year after his return from South America, Le Corbusier was engaged again to design a house in Buenos Aires: an urban villa for Julián Martinez.[17] The contact with Martinez had come through Victoria Ocampo. Contrary to what had happened with the house for Ocampo, Le Corbusier devoted more attention to this small project. It achieved a rather complete development at the schematic design level, with strong resemblances to some of his domestic masterpieces of previous years, such as the Villas Stein-de Monzie and Savoye. In December 1930, Le Corbusier sent Mr. Martinez a letter and a set of drawings with the project for his house.[18] The same day he wrote to Antonio Vilar, one of his architect friends from Buenos Aires, who, through an agreement made during Le Corbusier's previous visit to Buenos Aires, was to supervise the construction and execution of Le Corbusier's projects in Argentina. However, as with the Ocampo projects, this house was never realized.

MAISON CURUTCHET

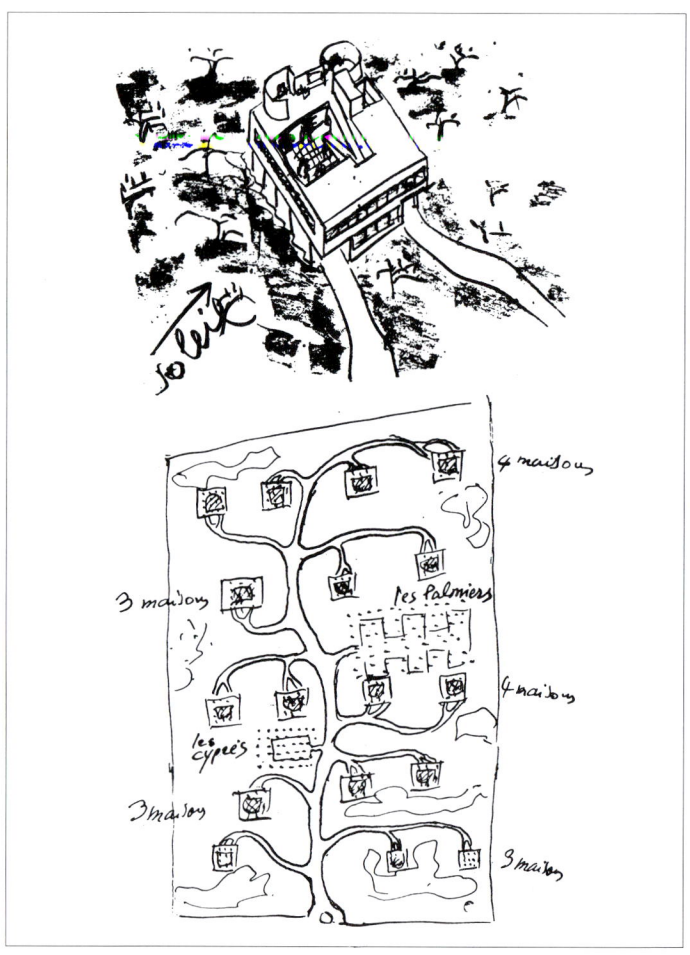

FIG 3. Residential weekend complex near the Delta. Sketch project, Tigre, 1929.

INTRODUCTION

FIG 4. Villa Ocampo project, Buenos Aires, 1928.
Model reconstruction by Gustavo Benvenuto and Ricardo Isaurralde.

FIG 5. Villa Martinez project, Buenos Aires, 1930. Model reconstruction by Gonzalo Etchegorry.

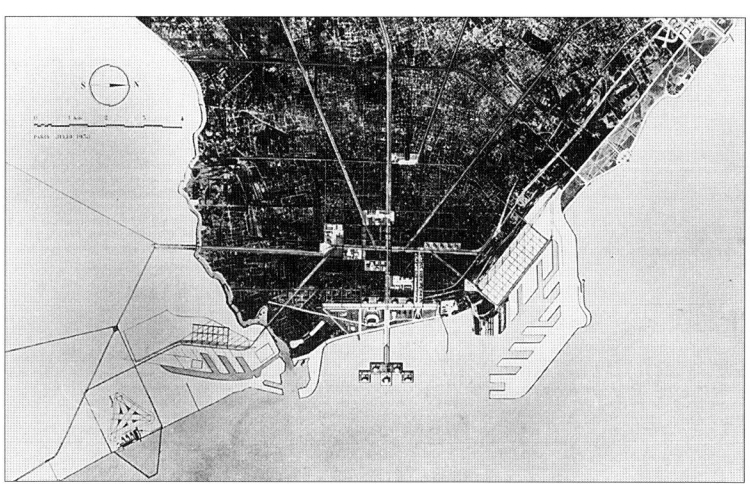

FIG 6. Le Corbusier's master plan for Buenos Aires, 1938-39.

INTRODUCTION

The next project Le Corbusier undertook for Argentina was, in terms of its scope, the most important: the 1938 Plan Directeur de Buenos Aires. In July 1937, Jorge Ferrari Hardoy and Juan Kurchan, who had recently graduated in architecture from the Universidad de Buenos Aires, collaborated with Le Corbusier at his Parisian atelier in producing a master plan for Buenos Aires. It must be clearly understood that there was no commission from the city of Buenos Aires for the development of this plan. Rather, it was Le Corbusier's own initiative, a dream that had begun in 1929 when he visited the city for the first (and only) time. Nevertheless, Le Corbusier had great hopes and expectations for this project. From an urban planning point of view, it was a chance to finally realize some of his ideas on city design. On a more personal basis, he hoped that the Plan Directeur would stimulate additional architectural commissions from Buenos Aires, particularly the most important architectural component of his proposal: the Cité des Affaires, or business district.[19]

The complete story of the Buenos Aires planning affair is not essential in understanding the design of Maison Curutchet. However, it is important to briefly review this event for the role it might have played in Dr. Curutchet's selection of Le Corbusier to design his house, as well as in the architect's decision to accept the commission. For many years Le Corbusier sent letters to his influential friends in Argentina, insisting on carrying out the plan, or at least making an official publication of this work, which he, nonetheless, had already included in a reduced version in the third volume of his *Oeuvre Complète*.[20]

Le Corbusier's aspirations for his 1938-39 Plan Directeur finally seemed feasible when, in December 1947, the Municipality of Buenos Aires created a committee for its study. The committee included Jorge Ferrari Hardoy as executive counselor and three other members, all "young architects of ideas CIAM."[21] Ferrari Hardoy proposed a two-phase plan of action and nominated Le Corbusier as advisor to the committee.[22] Le Corbusier accepted, but not without insisting on being commissioned "in the meantime" to design an important building for Buenos Aires.[23] In 1948 the government held long discussions, which were widely covered by the local press, concerning the implementation of the Plan. It was precisely in the middle of these discussions, in September 1948, and probably prompted by the continuous reference in the media to Le Corbusier's modern ideas, that Dr. Curutchet decided to contact the Parisian architect. Le Corbusier accepted this commission immediately despite its small size and distant location, probably hoping that through the resolution of this little house, he could demonstrate his urban and architectural principles and thus persuade the Buenos Aires legislature to approve his master plan for the city.

In 1949 the relationship between Le Corbusier and Ferrari Hardoy deteriorated however, and finally in November 1949, long after the design of Maison Curutchet had been completed, the committee for the study of Le Corbusier's Plan de Buenos Aires was dissolved. One month earlier, on October 10, 1949, Le Corbusier, frustrated, had written bitterly to Ferrari Hardoy: "As far as I am concerned, I have received from Argentina one of the most deceptive gestures of my entire career. . . . [Buenos Aires] is the city without hope, the catastrophic city that I very well know."[24] Thus ended the story of the Plan de Buenos Aires. Once again, as with those projects for Madame Ocampo and Julián Martinez, nothing was built.

In the forties Le Corbusier had had other contacts with Argentina. Between 1942 and 1944 he collaborated with *Tecné,* an Argentinean professional review dedicated to architecture and urbanism. Richard Neutra, Edgar Kaufmann, Eduardo Sacriste, Ferrari Hardoy, Juan Kurchan, and Antonio Bonet, were also collaborators of this review that was directed by Conrado Sondereguer and Simón Ungar.

The final episode in the professional relationship between Le Corbusier and Argentina took place in the late fifties and early sixties when Guido Di Tella, an Argentine industrialist, attempted to obtain Le Corbusier's services as architect on two occasions. The first time Di Tella contacted Le Corbusier, he hoped to obtain his participation in the design of the administrative headquarters of SIAM-Di Tella Ltda, a large local industrial holding.[25] A short time later Di Tella tendered a new proposal: the design of an art institute that would bear the name of his father, the industrialist Torcuato Di Tella.[26] Le Corbusier did not respond favorably to either of the two possibilities, claiming that he was extremely busy. However, Di Tella insisted once again by appealing to the artist in Le Corbusier. He organized a gathering of one-hundred and fifty painters, sculptors, art critics and art collectors at Lirolay, an art gallery in Buenos Aires, to sign a document in support of his project: "A Building by Le Corbusier in Buenos Aires." Among them were Le Corbusier's friends, the sculptor Pablo Curatella-Manés and his wife Germaine Derbecq, and the most important representatives of the local artistic and intellectual community.[27] This was the last time Le Corbusier had professional contact

INTRODUCTION

with Argentina, and like all but one of his experiences there, it ended without a built outcome.

Pablo Curatella-Manés, who died in Buenos Aires in 1962, and his wife Germaine continued to keep Le Corbusier informed of the architectural and artistic activity in Buenos Aires. They, Amancio Williams and, to an extent, Victoria Ocampo were the long-standing friends Le Corbusier maintained in the country that in the late twenties had embraced his avant-garde ideas, but later turned from his urban prophecies, dreams and ambitions. It was Dr. Curutchet, someone who did not belong to the Buenos Aires avant-garde, who materialized the only building of the many that Le Corbusier had designed for sites in Argentina.

NOTES

1   Comisión Nacional de Museos, Monumentos y Lugares Históricos.
2   William Curtis, *Le Corbusier, Ideas and Forms* (New York: Rizzoli, 1986), 225.
3   See, for example, Curtis, *Le Corbusier, Ideas and Forms*, and Stanislaus von Moos, *Le Corbusier, Elements of a Synthesis* (Cambridge: MIT Press, 1985).
4   William Boesiger and Hans Girsberger, *Le Corbusier 1910-65* (New York and Washington: Frederick A. Praeger, 1967), 82-83. It was Le Corbusier's habit to republish a building in newer volumes of the *Oeuvre Complète* if completion had been achieved after its initial publication as a project. This was not the case with Maison Curutchet, however, which—even after it was completed, and photographs had been sent to him before the publication of newer volumes—remained merely a project within the architect's publication of his "complete works."
5   In fact, the building was published after its completion in some international architectural publications. Photographs of the finished building, including Le Corbusier's drawings, were published in an issue of *Architectural Design* dedicated to the modern house. "Argentina: House of Dr. Curutchet at La Plata," *Architectural Design* 3 (March, 1956): 86-88. A comparable publication of the house was included in Henry Russell-Hitchcock, *Latin American Architecture since 1945* (New York: The Museum of Modern Art, 1955), 158-161.
6   For example: Roger Aujame, "Maison du Dr. Curutchet à La Plata, 1949," *Techniques et Architecture* 373 (September, 1987): 52-55; Andrés Duprat, "Le Corbusier australe: casa Curutchet a La Plata," *Casabella* 573 (November, 1990): 24-26; and James Warren, "Preservation: Corb in Context," *Progressive Architecture* (April, 1989): 22.
7   The Ministry of Education and Public Health constructed in Rio de Janeiro, Brazil, in 1936 is unmistakably a Corbusian building, but it was designed in association with several young Brazilian architects (Lucio Costa, Oscar Niemeyer, Alfonso Reidy, Carlos Leao, Jorge Moreira and Ernani Vasconcelos).
8   Le Corbusier, *Precisions: on the present state of architecture and city planning*. Translated by Edith Schreiber Aujame. (Cambridge, MA: MIT Press, 1991), 18.
9   Among the cultural activities organized by Amigos del Arte were the exhibitions of artists like

David Alfaro Siqueiros, Emilio Petorutti, Lino Eneas Spilimbergo and Pablo Curatella-Manés; a lecture series with José Ortega y Gasset, Le Corbusier and Leopoldo Lugones; music sessions by the Cuarteto Aguilar and tango music; and a presentation of films by Sergei Eisenstein. "Le Corbusier en Buenos Aires, 1929," *Revista de la Sociedad Central de Arquitectos*, (1979): 9.

10 Laura Ayerza del Castillo and Odile Felgine, *Victoria Ocampo* (Paris: Editorial Criterion, 1991), 114-115.

11 Le Corbusier, *Precisions*, 4.

12 *Precisions: on the present state of architecture and city planning*, the reelaborated transcript of the South American lectures, is preceded by an "American Prologue," and includes an appendix that contains two short, contemporaneous essays: "The Temperature of Paris," and "The Atmosphere of Moscow."

13 Pancho Liernur and Pablo Pschepiurca, "Precisiones sobre los proyectos de Le Corbusier en la Argentina 1929/1949," *Summa* 243 (November, 1987): 45-46. Liernur and Pschepiurca have written some of the most interesting and insightful essays and criticism of Le Corbusier's work in Argentina.

14 Ernesto Katzenstein, "Argentine Architecture of the Thirties," *DAPA, Journal of Decorative Arts* (1992): 54-75.

15 Katzenstein, "Argentine Architecture," 59.

16 Le Corbusier; *Precisions*, 139

17 In the 32 volumes of *The Le Corbusier Archive* (London and Paris: Garland Publishing and La Fondation Le Corbusier, 1983-84), there are four houses designed by Le Corbusier for sites in Argentina: Villa Ocampo (1928, vol. 5), and the Villas Curutchet, Martinez, and Paulo Prado (1949, vol. 19). However, the purist language of Villa Martinez seems unlikely to belong to the late forties, and fits better within the Corbusian language of the late twenties and early thirties. Furthermore, letters addressed to Antonio Vilar and to Julián Martinez on December 3, 1930, with a brief description of the Martinez house correspond with the drawings published in *The Le Corbusier Archive* (vol. 19, 310-330). In regard to the Villa Paulo Prado, it is unlikely that this house was located in Buenos Aires as it is indicated in *The Le Corbusier Archive*. As Paulo Prado was a Brazilian millionaire, it is more likely that his project would had been located in Brazil. Surely, these were two involuntary "misplacements" incurred during the overwhelming task of compiling the totality of Le Corbusier's architectural drawings.

18 Le Corbusier to Julián Martinez, 3 December 1930, Fondation Le Corbusier, Paris; Dossier Julián Martinez (FLC 11-17): 15-17.

19 For an extensive treatment of the Plan Directeur de Buenos Aires, see *La Arquitectura de Hoy* 4 (April, 1947). See also Manuel Borthagaray, Jorge Glusberg, and Benoit Junot, *Le Corbusier y Buenos Aires, el Plan Regulador, 1938-40*, (Buenos Aires: Cayc Publications, 1981); and Liernur and Pschepiurca, "Precisiones sobre los proyectos."

20 Le Corbusier and Max Bill, *Oeuvre Complète 1934-1938*, 2nd edition. (Zurich: Editions Girsberger, 1945): 58-59.

21 Ferrari Hardoy to Le Corbusier 11 March, 1948, Fondation Le Corbusier, Paris; Dossier Plan de Buenos Aires (FLC T2-13): 31.

22 Ibid., and transcript of a Municipality of Buenos Aires Decree, Dossier Plan de Buenos Aires (FLC T2-13): 27-32.

23 Le Corbusier to Ferrari Hardoy, 25 March 1948, Dossier Plan de Buenos Aires (FLC T2-13): 37.

24 Le Corbusier to Ferrari Hardoy, 10 October 1949, Dossier Plan de Buenos Aires (FLC T2-13): 36.

INTRODUCTION

25 Di Tella to Le Corbusier, 3 February 1960, Fondation Le Corbusier, Paris; Dossier Projet Guido Di Tella (FLC U2-13): 98.

26 Di Tella to Le Corbusier, 21 February 1960, Dossier Projet Guido Di Tella (FLC U2-13): 99.

27 These included Silvina Ocampo (Victoria's sister), Manuel Mujica Lainez, Enio Iommi, Antonio Berni, Libero Badii, Marta Minujin, Carlos Cortese, Manu Martorell, Graciela Rodo, Kemble, and others. It is not known if Le Corbusier ever worked on a project for Di Tella. The correspondence between Di Tella and Le Corbusier, including the long signed document of the gathering at Lirolay, rests today in a file at the Fondation Le Corbusier entitled "Projet Guido Di Tella; construction par Le Corbusier d'une musée-centre d'Art pour y habiter les collections de la Fondation Di Tella, Buenos Aires 1961," Dossier Projet Guido Di Tella (FLC U2-13).

Let us state the problem. A house: a shelter against heat, cold, rain, thieves and the inquisitive. A receptacle for light and sun. A certain number of cells appropriated to cooking, work, and personal life.

—Le Corbusier, *Towards a New Architecture*, 114

CHAPTER I

THE COMMISSION

The events related to the realization of Maison Curutchet are rather unusual, not only because of the personalities involved, but also because of the circumstances that determined its commission, design and construction. One of the most interesting aspects in the history of the house is the relationship between the client, Dr. Pedro Curutchet, and the architect, Le Corbusier, and their striking similarities: they both shared explosive personalities, as well as an interest and belief in the potential benefits of modern life. Dr. Curutchet's unsurpassed respect for Le Corbusier's plastic and artistic achievement constitutes a very rare case in professional and personal relationships, and presents a key to a critical understanding of the house.

Another curious factor in the story behind the house is Le Corbusier's motivation to accept a commission from an unknown client. Considering that at the time his atelier was almost fully dedicated to the Unité d'Habitation in Marseilles, why did Le Corbusier accept such a small commission from a distant country? Undoubtedly, Le Corbusier's serious intentions to materialize his urban proposals in Buenos Aires influenced his acceptance of the commission. The involvement of Amancio Williams, one of the most important and capable exponents of modern architecture in Latin America, is yet another relevant element of the building's history. Williams was responsible for producing construction documents, and supervised the first phase of construction of the house. More than merely a supervisor, however, Williams played a key role in the eventual realization of the project despite its many setbacks, and is the primary party responsible for the way the building was translated from design to built work.

Finally, the numerous turns and obstacles that Dr. Curutchet confronted and eventually overcame throughout the process (from before the first line had been drawn in Paris, until six years later, when he and his family moved into the house), his often conflictive relationship with the site architects

FIG 7. Dr. Pedro Domingo Curutchet in front of his recently completed house.

(Williams first, Simón Ungar later), the family's unexpected short-lived occupation of the house, and, more recently, the renovation and declaration of the house as a national monument, are other aspects that contribute to the building's unusual history.

Dr. Curutchet and the Commission of Maison Curutchet

Dr. Pedro Domingo Curutchet was born on April 2, 1901, in Las Flores, a small town located 112 miles south of the city of Buenos Aires, in the heart of the rich Province of Buenos Aires. He spent his youth in La Plata, the capital of the Province of Buenos Aires, where he attended medical school and graduated in the mid-1920s. He was a well-read and erudite man who embraced broad cultural interests, particularly in the domains of music, literature, design, painting, and contemporary art, to the extent that he helped finance a journal on graphic art.[1] His life-style was austere, he never liked to travel, and he preferred to spend his time reading. In later years he liked to define himself as a solitary person who enjoyed humor and laughter.[2]

In 1930 he settled down in the small town of Lobería, 370 miles from La Plata and Buenos Aires, where he practiced medicine as a rural physician and surgeon, implementing—in such adverse conditions—a surprisingly successful method of home surgery. A self-consciously "modern" man, Dr. Curutchet researched innovative and more efficient methods and materials to apply to his field. He was one of the first in the world to point out that a surgeon's hands must be comfortable in order to operate well, and that there is an optimal "functional position" that must be respected for the hands to work most effectively and comfortably.[3] In effect, as Dr. Joel Noé of Harvard Medical School explained, Dr. Curutchet's major contribution was his development of a new, innovative technique in surgery, which Dr. Curutchet called the "aximanual technique." He also designed aximanual instruments of surgery, which earned him international reputation in the field.

In the fifties and sixties he promoted this revolutionary surgical technique in two books entitled *Aximanual Surgery: Technology and History* and *Axitechnical Surgery and Crucimanual History*.[4] Throughout the two books, Dr. Curutchet demonstrated his interest in and knowledge of other fields, through analogies and allusions to art, literature, music and sports. By relating surgical issues to these other, "more respectable" fields, Curutchet was able to reinforce his arguments and thus advance his own innovations. This technique of borrowing from other arts is one Le Corbusier himself often

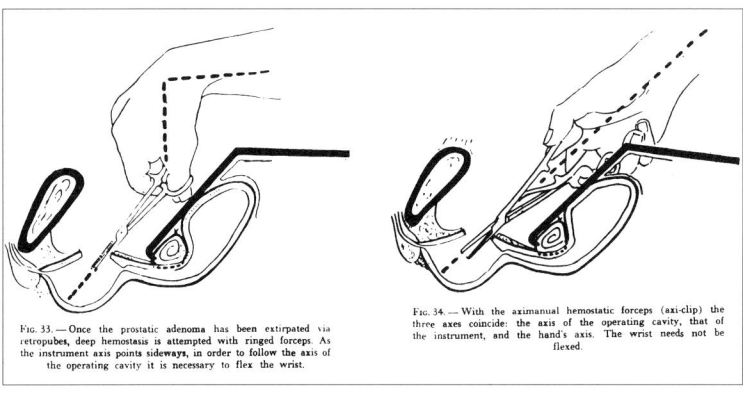

FIG. 33.—Once the prostatic adenoma has been extirpated via retropubes, deep hemostasis is attempted with ringed forceps. As the instrument axis points sideways, in order to follow the axis of the operating cavity it is necessary to flex the wrist.

FIG. 34.—With the aximanual hemostatic forceps (axi-clip) the three axes coincide: the axis of the operating cavity, that of the instrument, and the hand's axis. The wrist needs not be flexed.

FIG 8. Drawing comparing the traditional "crucimanual surgical technique" to Curutchet's "aximanual technique," and the aximanual instruments he designed.

used. The bibliographical references include works by Eugène Delacroix, Nelly Sachs, Maurice Maeterlinck and even Mathyla Ghyka's book on the golden section. References to Igor Stravinsky, J.S. Bach, Paul Valéry, and others abound throughout the two volumes. The direct and insistent tone of his writing style is reminiscent of Le Corbusier's own written work.

In effect, like Le Corbusier, Dr. Curutchet firmly believed in the benefits of modern times. Thus, as Argentinean critics Pancho Liernur and Pablo Pschepiurca have noted, Dr. Curutchet represented "a suggestive 'subject of modernity' very compatible with the Corbusian myths of the modern man."[5]

In 1948, Curutchet decided to move back to La Plata, where he had acquired a very small plot of land facing a beautiful park. He wanted a house in which he could also establish a clinic for the practice of his revolutionary surgical methods. Looking for an architect who could interpret his needs appropriately, he wrote to an architect in Buenos Aires outlining his needs, but received no answer.[6] In later years he insisted that he could not remember the architect's name, but recalled that his work was frequently published in the magazine *Casas y Jardines*.[7] Frustrated, and attributing the lack of an answer to the arrogance of architects from Buenos Aires, he decided to contact Le Corbusier. He was not certain what prompted him to do so, but in a letter to Jorge Silvetti he attributed the decision to a "good sudden idea":

> ... if I would answer your question why I asked Le Corbusier to design my house, I would not be certain to explain it, it happened a long time ago. Maybe because, as Baltazar Gracián wrote, "one has good sudden ideas." Sometimes, I ask myself the same question, and I suspect that it was because I had an affinity with the great innovator [Le Corbusier], being in my own way a revolutionary architect of surgical instruments and technique.[8]

He also recalled that after the lack of response from the first architect he had contacted, he gave more thought to his proposal and concluded that his site and program "could be better explored by a modern architect, a man with the ideas of Le Corbusier."[9] He had never met Le Corbusier, nor had he any contact with Le Corbusier's Argentinean friends. He thus asked his sister Leonor, who traveled frequently to Europe, to visit Le Corbusier's atelier in Paris and ask him to design his house and clinic in La Plata. Thus, client and architect were not going to meet, and in fact, they never did meet, nor did they ever have a personal conversation. Their professional relationship was to remain indirect and fairly impersonal, conducted strictly by mail and through third parties, establishing a rather unusual case in client-architect relationships.

In September 1948, Leonor traveled to Paris in the company of their mother, and carried with her an information package containing photographs of the site and a detailed program of Dr. Curutchet's needs. On September 3, they visited the architect's atelier at 35 rue de Sèvres. Their initial impression was very disappointing: Le Corbusier's office was a crowded corridor on the top floor of a former convent. It was precisely the opposite of what they had expected from the master of modern architecture, whose ideas about large, open, clean and hygienic spaces they had come to know through the Argentinean press.[10] Nevertheless, the two women met with Le Corbusier and gave him the site photographs and the long document outlining the programmatic requirements for Dr. Curutchet's house and clinic.

That same day Le Corbusier made quick calculations on the square footage, cost of construction, and his professional fee. The size of the house was estimated as 531 square meters, and the cost, 300 Argentinean pesos per square meter.[11] The total cost was then estimated to be 150,000 pesos (approximately 31,365 dollars at that time). On September 7, only four days after he had met with Leonor Curutchet, Le Corbusier sent a note to her hotel in Paris which included a letter addressed to Dr. Curutchet accepting the commission. In the same letter the architect established his three conditions: (1) he would design a preliminary project in accordance with the program requirements and send it to Dr. Curutchet for his evaluation; after review he would then define a final project; (2) his honorarium would be fixed at 10 per cent of the total cost of the house;[12] and (3) the construction of the house would be supervised by one of Le Corbusier's Argentinean friends—he would later provide a list of possible names, and Curutchet would choose among them.

Once his conditions were clearly established, Le Corbusier concluded his letter with a statement that outlined his personal interest and intentions for this work:

> ... I will undertake this work with pleasure, given that your project is characteristic of a small residential house, which has always interested me. Your program: the house of a physician, is extremely seductive (from a social point of view). Your site is well located, and offers favorable conditions. In short, having established a plan for Buenos Aires in 1938-39, which is currently being considered by the government, I am interested in producing for you a small masterpiece of

simplicity, conformity and harmony, all within the limitations of an extremely simple construction with no luxuries, as is typical of my work.[13]

Leonor Curutchet immediately sent the letter to her brother. Dr. Curutchet answered promptly on September 16, and posed some questions concerning professional fees and procedures.[14] Again, Le Corbusier responded immediately, on September 28, with another three-point letter. The first point clarified that his honorarium, as established in his previous letter, did not include an honorarium for supervision and management of construction. The second point, the most important of the letter, listed the names and addresses of four architects that Le Corbusier recommended for construction supervision. The third point determined the procedural forms of payment.[15]

The four choices Le Corbusier suggested for construction supervisor were Amancio Williams, the team of Kurchan & Ferrari Hardoy, Antonio Bonet and Carlos Gomez Gavazzo. All of them had well-established, yet clearly different relationships with the European architect. Amancio Williams, the first on the list, was a young architect from Buenos Aires who had earned a particular and unusual respect from Le Corbusier. Juan Kurchan and Jorge Ferrari Hardoy had worked with Le Corbusier in 1938 and 1939 in the development of the unsolicited master plan for Buenos Aires and then became deeply involved in the political process of its possible implementation; they also maintained an important practice in Buenos Aires. Antonio Bonet, who had collaborated on some projects with Kurchan & Ferrari Hardoy, was originally from Spain and was also involved in the Plan de Buenos Aires as well as a CIAM representative for Argentina; his work in Uruguay was, at that time, often published in the periodical *L'Architecture d'Aujourd'hui*. Gomez Gavazzo was a professor of architecture in Montevideo, where he also had a well-established practice and reputation as a modern rationalist architect, and was a personal friend of Le Corbusier. The letter did not indicate whether the names were listed in a hierarchical or preferential order. However, considering the relationship that Le Corbusier had with each of them at that particular time, the letter did list the names following a certain hierarchy.[16] It is uncertain whether Dr. Curutchet contacted all four candidates before making a decision, for virtually no documents about this process exist and the doctor refused to refer to it in later years. Perhaps his instinct interpreted Le Corbusier's order and directly asked Amancio Williams, the first on the list, to undertake construction supervision.

Amancio Williams was born in Buenos Aires in 1913 and is considered one of the most important modern architects of Argentina.[17] The house that he had designed and built for his father, the music composer Alberto Williams, internationally known as "Casa del Puente" ("Bridge House" or "House Over the Brook"), and other projects, had been published in *L'Architecture d'Aujourd'hui* in the mid-to-late forties. He had introduced himself and his work to Le Corbusier through a letter dated January 23, 1946.[18] Le Corbusier found Williams' work very attractive: "You are very talented. All this [Williams projects] breathes the air of the large seas and the pampas, providing us with a sense of space and decision. . ."[19] He also requested Williams' consent to submit part of the documentation to André Wogensky, then director of the journal *L'Homme et l'Architecture*, for publication. Le Corbusier then committed himself to writing an article on Williams' work.[20] Such a response was the beginning of a good personal and professional relationship between Williams and Le Corbusier that, however distanced by the large seas, would continue for the rest of their lives.

Dr. Curutchet communicated his decision of selecting Williams to Le Corbusier in a letter dated October 12, 1948.[21] Dr. Curutchet had also requested further details regarding the method of payment and whether Le Corbusier's honorarium of 15,000 pesos (10 per cent of the estimated cost of construction) would be increased if the final cost of the house exceeded the estimated amount. This concern was a clear reference to the effects of inflation that were then affecting Argentina's economy. Le Corbusier decided then to fix his honorarium in American dollars equal to 15,000 pesos at the exchange rate of that day;[22] thus, his honorarium would not be increased in pesos as a result of Argentina's inflation, but by fixing it in dollars, it would be automatically adjusted to the natural inflation-caused devaluation of the peso.

This solution might have resolved the problem quite soon and simply. However, it was difficult for Dr. Curutchet to formalize the first payment of the honorarium as requested. Juan D. Perón was then president of Argentina and was in the process of implementing an aggressive program to nationalize the economy, which seems to have presented problems for Curutchet to formalize a deposit and/or payment in foreign currency. Dr. Curutchet wrote again to Le Corbusier on November 6 requesting other rules and regulations for payment.[23] Le Corbusier's response was to establish his honorarium at 2,954 dollars, and to deposit that amount in his account at the French Amer-

THE COMISSION

FIG 9. Amancio Williams, Suspended Office Building, project, 1946.

FIG 10. Amancio Williams, Casa del Puente in Mar del Plata, Argentina, 1943-45, exterior.

ican Banking Corporation in New York.[24] Apparently this solution was not feasible either, and in the end Curutchet proposed to deposit the total amount (not just the first half installment of the honorarium, as had been previously agreed) in an Argentinean account. Le Corbusier accepted, and instructed his client to deposit the said amount in the account of Comodoro Eduardo Chueca at the Banco Nación in Buenos Aires.[25] Le Corbusier also demanded to be notified by telegram as soon as the deposit had been made.[26]

Finally, on February 1, 1949, after a process of almost five months—perhaps a premonition of what was to come—Dr. Pedro D. Curutchet sent a telegram to Le Corbusier: the deposit had been executed. Le Corbusier acknowledged the telegram the next day, noting that he would begin the design work immediately and would try to finish the project as soon as possible.[27]

Site and Program

The material that Dr. Curutchet had sent to Le Corbusier through his sister Leonor had included a fairly complete package consisting of site data, site photographs, and a fifteen-page document describing his programmatic needs in great detail.[28] The site was located at the northeastern end of La Plata, the young capital of the Province of Buenos Aires. This city was only a few years old, having been founded in 1882 through the initiative of governor Dardo Rocha, as the new capital of the Province of Buenos Aires. The need for a new capital had emerged when the city of Buenos Aires became federalized in 1880, leaving the rich agricultural provincial state without its most important city and, more critically, without its essential port on the Rio de la Plata (a fundamental facility for the country's export-based economy). Thus, La Plata was founded not only as the provincial administrative seat, but also as a new port to compete with the one in Buenos Aires City, the country's capital and natural port. The new city, a wonderful combination of centralized and linear planning, was designed and built from a virtual tabula rasa by a committee that applied the latest developments in urban design and used the newest available technology. Its conception and layout represent a interesting case of late nineteenth-century urbanism:

> The perimeter of the city is a perfect square, bordered by a boulevard 100 meters wide that encloses an area of a square legua.[29] The general form of the city is made up of blocks measuring 120 meters square, and is bisected by two 30-meter-wide boulevards. Between these two boulevards, there are city blocks measuring 120 meters long; at either side of the boulevards there are blocks

THE COMISSION

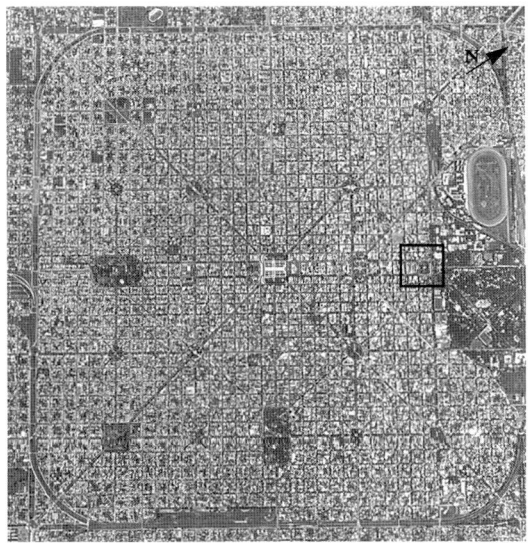

FIG 11. Aerial view of La Plata. Boxed area at right indicates location of Curutchet's site.

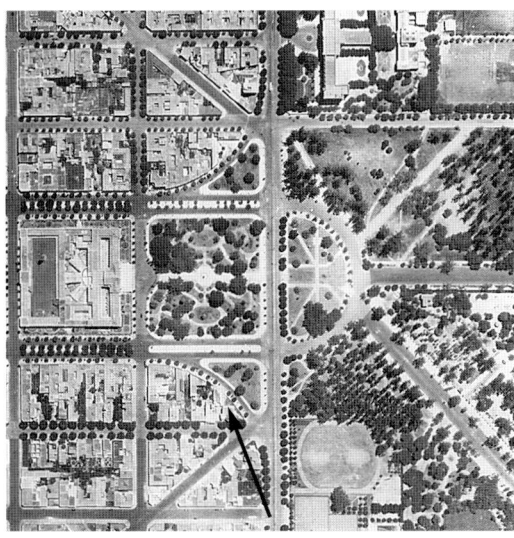

FIG 12. Detail showing the site of the Curutchet lot (denoted by arrow).

which, starting at 60 meters wide by 120 meters long, progressively increase in 10 meter increments until they reach the general size of 120 by 120 meters. Two 30-meter wide diagonals cross the city from one extreme to the other and six more diagonals connect the main plazas and the great parks.[30]

Dr. Curutchet's site is situated at the end of one of the two boulevards that divide the city at the center. More precisely, it is located on its northeastern side, where the boulevard, Calle N° 53, curves outward to meet Paseo del Bosque, a large urban park preceding an even larger green area that connects the perimeter of the city with the Rio de la Plata. The physical characteristics of the site are particularly complex: small and irregular, it measures almost nine meters wide by 22.75 meters deep on one side, and 17.25 meters deep on the other side (29 feet, 75 feet and 56.6 feet, respectively). The front of the lot is cut at a diagonal which parallels the street, and measures approximately 10.20 meters (33.5 feet). Furthermore, the plot is surrounded on three sides by existing buildings. The angled front side of the site faces Calle N° 53, beyond which the boulevard and the Paseo del Bosque open up to the wide horizons of the pampas.

Dr. Curutchet was particularly fond of these wide panoramic views of the landscape. Of the five photographs he sent to Le Corbusier of the site and its environs, three of them showed the park as seen from his lot looking west, north, and east. Together, they composed Dr. Curutchet's beloved view of the park. The other two photographs showed the site as seen from the east and west. Dr. Curutchet meticulously marked on the photographs the east-west axis with a dashed blue line, emphasizing that these two latter images were purposely taken to study extreme conditions of sunlight exposure. Furthermore, he reminded his architect of the importance of appropriate sunlight for living areas and bedrooms.[31]

In addition to emphasizing the importance of the view, Dr. Curutchet was also quite specific about his room requirements. He had patiently developed an extremely detailed and meticulous fifteen-page document. This document, which he suggestively entitled "Exposición Sumaria," or "Brief" also included clips from *La Arquitectura de Hoy*, and other journals illustrating furnishings of his preference.[32] Dr. Curutchet requested a medium-priced house for himself, his wife, and two young daughters, and asked that it include the following rooms: porch, hall, garage, living room (which should include separate areas for panoramic views of the landscape, fireplace, music area with a small piano, and writing desk), dining room (adjoining the living

THE COMISSION

FIG 13. View of the site from the east. Photograph sent by Dr. Curutchet to Le Corbusier. Note the dashed line (center right) indicating the exact east orientation.

FIG 14. View of the site from the west. Note the dashed line indicating the exact west orientation.

room and its fireplace), kitchen, breakfast, pantry, laundry, storage, three bedrooms and two bathrooms, and maid's quarters (bedroom, toilet and shower). His medical office, and related waiting room and toilet were also to be incorporated.

Curutchet clearly stated that the distribution of rooms was the responsibility of the architect. Nonetheless, he suggested the possibility of a three-level building as an appropriate solution: living and social areas on the ground floor, bedrooms on the upper level, and medical office, waiting room, and services in the basement. However, the most important aspect of Dr. Curutchet's program lay in the spirit of the document that stressed the beauty of the park, and clearly inspired a modern living style, where "comfort, practicality, easy maintenance and casual living are the principal things."[33] In fact, the panoramic view of the park and the boulevard, and appropriate natural lighting of the living and private areas were stressed as the most important aspects that the architect needed to address, ranked above any of his other needs. References to simple maintenance and cleaning, hygiene, and a careful consideration of appropriate levels of thermal and acoustic insulation abounded throughout the document. He also gave unusual attention to the avoidance of dust accumulation, a clear example of Dr. Curutchet's preoccupation with proper hygiene, in medicine in particular and in the contemporary world in general.[34] Interestingly, the rhetoric used by Dr. Curutchet to express his intentions and concerns was very similar to the architect's own writing, and probably contributed to Le Corbusier's acceptance of the commission.

In sum, while the site was well-located and offered attractive views of the beautiful park and boulevard, its dimensions were small and irregular. The program was interesting in itself "from a social point of view," and its intrinsic complexity demanded "a masterpiece of simplicity." The client himself was not unlike the Corbusian prototype of the modern man: he was sophisticated, open-minded, progressive and demanded the advantages of modern living. The difficult conditions imposed by this combination of site, program and client required an unusually intelligent and creative architectural solution. The design challenge posed by Maison Curutchet seemed especially tailored to Le Corbusier.

THE COMISSION

NOTES

1. Curutchet helped finance the magazine *A*, related to the so-called group "Arte Concreto." Liernur and Pschepiurca, "Precisiones sobre los proyectos," 51. Enio Iommi, author of the sculpture located in the ground floor of Maison Curutchet, was a member of this group.
2. "*Me gusta el humor y la risa, pero soy un solitario, huyo de la gente, me han dicho y lo creo, pero me disculpo con el óleo de Roualt 'Le dur metier du vivre,' una de sus figuras más atormentadas. Cada día prefiero más desconocer la realidad humana y la utopía, pero, solo desde luego, para poder vivir así, con menos riesgo.*" Dr. Curutchet to Jorge Silvetti, 16 June 1978, The Curutchet Collection, Francis Loeb Library, Harvard University Graduate School of Design.
3. Dr. Joel M. Noé to the author, 12 September 1990, Cambridge, MA. Dr. Noé, teaches plastic and reconstructive surgery at Harvard Medical School. Early in his career, he developed an interest in Dr. Curutchet's aximanual technique in surgery, and visited him in La Plata in the seventies. Later, Dr. Curutchet considered Dr. Noé the "head" of the "aximanual school." Dr. Curutchet to Derek C. Bok, President of Harvard University, (undated), The Curutchet Collection.
4. Curutchet, *Aximanual Surgery: technology and history* (Buenos Aires, 1974), and *Axitechnical Surgery and Crucimanual History,* (Buenos Aires, 1976).
5. Liernur and Pschepiurca, "Precisiones sobre los proyectos," 51.
6. Dr. Curutchet repeatedly refused to make public the name of such architect/s. In referring to the number of professionals contacted by Dr. Curutchet before he wrote to Le Corbusier, I have chosen to take the most direct source, that is Daniel Casoy's conversation with Dr. Curutchet; Daniel Casoy, "Le Corbusier en La Plata: Entrevista con el Doctor Curutchet," *Arquitecturas Bis* 43 (March, 1983): 2-10. However, it is interesting to note that other sources disagree with the number of architects that Dr. Curutchet contacted before writing to Le Corbusier. In a short article dedicated to Maison Curutchet on the occasion of Le Corbusier's death, Miguel Asencio refers to three Argentinean architects who did not respond to Dr. Curutchet's request; M. Asencio, "Homenaje a Le Corbusier," *Nuestra Arquitectura* (September, 1965): 15-22. In another short article written on the occasion of the reopening of the house in 1988, Victoria Solís refers to two architects from Buenos Aires; Victoria Solís, "Nueva Vida y Función para una casa insigne," *Clarín*, Friday, 24 June 1988, Suplemento Arquitectura, full-page article.
7. Casoy, "Entrevista," 4.
8. Curutchet to Silvetti, 16 June 1978, The Curutchet Collection.
9. Casoy, "Entrevista," 4.
10. Ms. Leonor Amalia Curutchet de Goggi, telephone conversation with the author, Buenos Aires, January 1991.
11. This was about 63 dollars at that time. Le Corbusier's estimate was based on the following floor-by-floor square footage: basement, 100 m²; ground floor, 175 m²; first floor, 98 m²; and second and third, each 79 m². Le Corbusier to Curutchet; Fondation Le Corbusier, Paris; Dossier Villa du Dr. Curutchet (FLC 12 07A): 28.
12. This 10% was comprised of one half of 5% for the cost of construction plus one half of 14% of the cost of interior equipment (which totals 9.5%). Le Corbusier himself rounded the figure to 10% for his honorarium). One half of this honorarium, 7500 pesos, would be paid before beginning work; the remaining 5% would be paid in two installments: 4% at the beginning of construction, and the remaining 1% once the actual cost of construction and equipment was determined. Le Corbusier to Curutchet, 7 September 1948, Dossier Villa du Dr. Curutchet (FLC 12 07): 31.

13 "Voilà les conditions dans lesquelles j'entreprendrais volontiers ce travail étant donné que votre problème est caractéristique de la petite maison d'habitation qui a toujours eveillé tout mon intérêt. Votre programme: habitation d'un médecin est extrêmement séduisant (point de vue social). Votre terrain est bien situé, dans de bonnes conditions. Enfin ayant établi le plan de Buenos Ayres en 1938-39 qui est actuellement pris en considération par le Gouvernement, je suis intéressé à l'idée de réaliser chez vous un petit chef d'oeuvre de simplicité, de convenances et d'harmonie tout en restant dans les limites d'une construction extrêmement simple et sans aucun luxe conformément d'ailleurs à mes habitudes." Ibid.
14 I have been unable to find this letter. However, this information can be inferred from Le Corbusier's answer of September 28.
15 Le Corbusier to Curutchet, 28 September 1948, Dossier Villa du Dr. Curutchet (FLC 12 07): 32. It is interesting to note that Antonio Vilar, who in 1929 had agreed to supervise the work of Le Corbusier in Argentina, was not included on the list. His name had been omitted previously during work on the Plan de Buenos Aires.
16 Le Corbusier was surely comfortable with the professionalism and commitment to modern architecture of all four architects listed. However, for either practical or personal reasons (or both) he had his own preferences. Gomez Gavazzo was a good friend and committed professional but he was based in Montevideo, Uruguay, too far from the construction site; thus, he was listed last. Of the remaining three, all based in Buenos Aires, he had a more fluent personal relationship with Williams and Kurchan & Ferrari Hardoy than with Bonet; thus the Spaniard was placed third. On a personal level Le Corbusier knew Kurchan and Ferrari Hardoy much better than Williams. The team had worked in his atelier, and they were still in contact through the ongoing discussions of his Plan de Buenos Aires. Although Le Corbusier was already frustrated and discouraged by the latest developments in the Plan, as a professional strategy he did not want to completely end his association with Kurchan and Ferrari Hardoy. Thus, Le Corbusier included their names on the list but only in second place. First place was reserved for Amancio Williams who, through correspondence begun only two years earlier, had earned Le Corbusier's warm respect as a quality architect.
17 The best source for the work of Amancio Williams is the book entitled *Amancio Williams*, edited by his own son Claudio Williams (Buenos Aires: Archivo Amancio Williams, 1990). For a good overview in English see: Jorge. Silvetti, ed., *Amancio Williams* (New York: Rizzoli, 1987). See also, Gianni Rigoli, "The Work of Amancio Williams," in *Zodiac* 16 (1966): 37-68.
18 Williams' submission included a brief autobiography, an account of his discovery of Le Corbusier's work and writing, and a small portfolio of the work produced in his *taller*. Williams to Le Corbusier, 23 January 1946, Fondation Le Corbusier, Dossier Amancio Williams (FLC R3-07): 201.
19 Le Corbusier to Williams, 9 April 1946, Dossier Amancio Williams (FLC E2 02): 61.
20 Le Corbusier's article was published in 1947. However, rather than a discussion of Williams' work, it consisted of a one-line introduction to the work of the architect after a page-long plea reaffirming the benefits and potential brought by modern times. Le Corbusier, "Amancio Williams," *L'Homme et l'Architecture* 15-16 (1947): 23.
21 I have been unable to find this letter in the archives. This information is inferred from Le Corbusier's answer dated to 28 October 1948.
22 Le Corbusier to Curutchet, 28 October 1948, The Curutchet Collection.
23 Letter also lost or unavailable; information inferred from Le Corbusier's answer.

THE COMISSION

24 Le Corbusier to Curutchet, 29 November 1948, Dossier Correspondence Le Corbusier (FLC G3 12): 20.
25 It is not known how Le Corbusier received the payment, and the nature of his relationship with Commodore E. Chueca is uncertain.
26 Le Corbusier to Curutchet, 19 January 1949, The Curutchet Collection.
27 Telegram unavailable. Information inferred from Le Corbusier's letter the following day, which acknowledged its receipt and committed himself to work on the project immediately. Le Corbusier to Curutchet, 2 Febrary 1949, The Curutchet Collection.
28 The document, written by Dr. Curutchet, bears the title "Futura Casa del Dr. Curutchet a Construirse en La Plata; Exposición Sumaria," Dossier Villa du Dr. Curutchet: (FLC 12 07 A): 36-49. Hereafter cited as "Exposición Sumaria."
29 A *legua* is an old Spanish unit equivalent to 5572.70 meters (3.46 miles).
30 Pedro Benoit, "Descripción de la Traza," taken from *a/mbiente* 32 (June, 1982): 30.
31 "Exposición Sumaria," 36.
32 Among the clippings included, it is interesting to mention a folding partition from a house in Pittsburgh designed by Walter Gropius and Marcel Breuer, which Curutchet proposed as a division between living and dining rooms. Ibid., 37.
33 Ibid., 48.
34 In fact, Dr. Curutchet's aximanual surgical theory was based on three interdependent elements: anesthesia, antisepsis (hygiene), and technique. Curutchet, *Aximanual Surgery*, 101.

... *a house is built with workmen and materials, and whether it is a success or the reverse depends on its plan and cross section.*
—Le Corbusier, *Oeuvre Complète*, vol. 1, 13

CHAPTER II

THE DESIGN PROCESS

When Le Corbusier accepted the commission from Dr. Curutchet, he and his team of young collaborators were already extremely busy with an influx of postwar building projects. Largely consumed by the design for the Unité d'Habitation in Marseilles, the atelier was also working on the Duval Factory at Saint Dié, and on the master plan for that same city. Le Corbusier himself was in the final stages of writing *Le Modulor*, and had begun work on *The Poem of the Right Angle*.[1] It would appear that Curutchet's commission—so far away in Argentina and such a small project in comparison to the large-scale building complexes he was already working on—would be easy to turn down at this busy time in Le Corbusier's career. However, despite these seeming detractions, he accepted it. He was not only interested and "seduced" by the program for Maison Curutchet, but also interested in the possible influence that this project could have toward implementing his Plan Directeur for Buenos Aires. Moreover, as Jerzy Soltan (who worked in the atelier when Maison Curutchet was designed) pointed out, Le Corbusier was "a man full of boyish eagerness to try everything to win a commission, a tempting piece of work, an exciting project."[2] Undoubtedly, Dr. Curutchet's commission inspired Le Corbusier in this way.

Because the atelier was completely occupied with the Unité project, Le Corbusier needed help to take on the design of Maison Curutchet. Thus, on February 2, 1949, the same day he received notification that his salary had been deposited in full, he sent a letter to Roger Aujame, a former collaborator who was then working at the Unité's site in Marseilles, requesting his return to the atelier to work on Maison Curutchet's project.[3] The "Curutchet team" was completed by Bernard Hoesli, a young architect who had recently joined the atelier.[4]

The design process formally started on February 4, 1949, that is, two days after Le Corbusier had responded to Dr. Curutchet and summoned Aujame to work on the project. The team Aujame-Hoesli established "camp" at the end of the corridor-like studio, near the mural designed by Le Corbusier. In the initial days of the process, the team worked intensively, developing the project from very small drawings that Le Corbusier had sketched to explain the volumetric and organizational principles of his idea. Aujame recalled that the task of interpreting these sketches was difficult due to the spatial complexity of the scheme, so they resorted to building test models from which they could then transcribe their findings into architectural drawings.[5] The architect sat with them at the end of each day, after supervising the ongoing work on the Unité d'Habitation, to review and further develop the project. Aujame recalled that Le Corbusier was confident of his initial concept for the project, but, nonetheless, he wanted to try other alternatives to make sure that the "direction" was correct, and that no doubts would arise.[6] Only a few days after the design process had begun, Le Corbusier wrote to Dr. Curutchet requesting further and more precise site information, particularly the characteristics of neighboring buildings.[7] This information would eventually become fundamental to the spatial and volumetric resolution of the building.

Considering the complexity of the program and the smallness of the site, Le Corbusier's objective, "to realize a small masterpiece of simplicity, convenience and harmony, within the limits of an extremely simple construction,"[8] was no easy task. The key to the project's resolution would be an intricate sequence of volumes interrelated by vertical open shafts that simultaneously separated, articulated, and gave architectural cohesiveness to the whole. In other words, Le Corbusier understood from the outset that the success of the project depended upon appropriate planning of the floor levels (recalling his maxim "the plan is the generator"), as well as on the spatial relationship among those levels as determined by the longitudinal section through the site.

Genesis and Development: Le Corbusier, Aujame and Hoesli at work
As many authors have indicated, it was Le Corbusier's modus operandi to let the problem occupy his mind for some time before the actual drafting process began, a time that Le Corbusier himself referred to as a period of "incubation of the idea."[9] This is what probably happened in the long months between the acceptance of the commission in September 1948, and the start of the design process in early February 1949, for by the time

design work had actually begun, the essential elements of the composition were already clearly established.

The design process started with the development of clay models, a technique often used at the atelier to develop, inform and annotate drawings.[10] Jerzy Soltan, who was then working on the project for Saint Dié and sat adjacent to Aujame and Hoesli in the atelier, recalled the beginning of the design of Maison Curutchet:

> . . . from its outset [it] became a typical model-leading case. The lot was small and tight. The plan had to rely on a vertical organization. The other planning trump cards were terraces and brise-soleils. Distributing spaces (open and enclosed) on the numerous levels, connecting them with ramps and staircases, and covering them with different types of roofs, ceilings, and flying slabs became the main themes of the spatial game. The relations between solids and voids, orthogonal and slanting, were very complex indeed. To develop these relationships on paper using standard projection techniques was impossible.[11]

These schematic models helped Hoesli and Aujame to see, and therefore understand, the complex spatial sequence that Le Corbusier had envisioned, especially the relationship between the medical clinic and the family dwelling.[12]

On February 8 Le Corbusier developed the first full-drawn version of the project (see FIG 15). These drawings, however schematic at that early stage in the design development, already included the most important and distinctive elements of the project:
- the ground floor dedicated to access and traffic (pedestrian and vehicular)
- the clinic on the first floor at the front of the site, and the residence enclosed in an elevated cubical volume to the rear of the site
- an outdoor ramp which simultaneously connected and separated house and clinic
- vertical shafts "carved out" of the virtual volume of the site, bringing additional natural light and ventilation
- a roof-garden opening off the living room, which resolved the rectangular shape of the house with the angled street front, as well as visually connecting the house to the park beyond
- a series of fins indicating a protective brise-soleil at the front of the site,

MAISON CURUTCHET

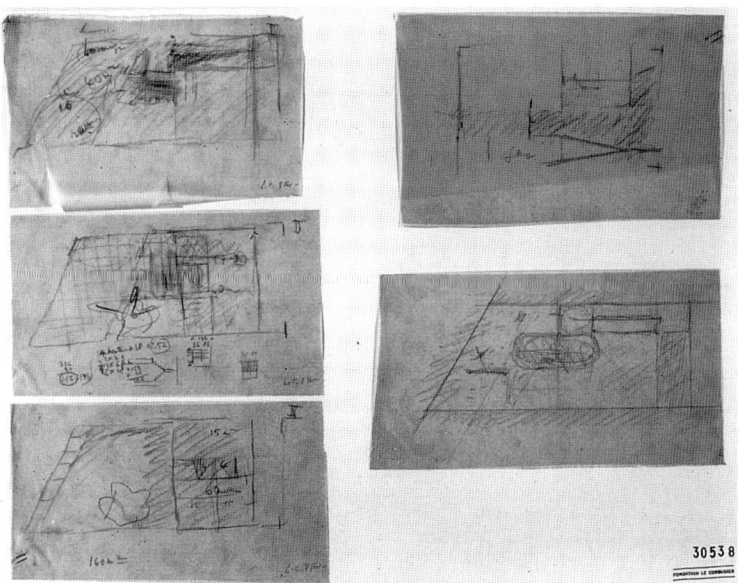

FIG 15. Le Corbusier's first, full-drafted version of the
Maison Curutchet, February 8, 1949. (FLC 30538)

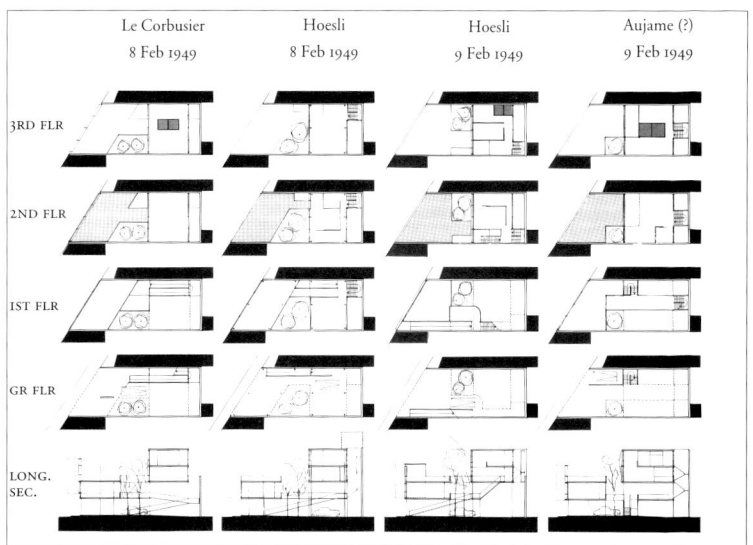

FIG 16. Reconstruction by the author of four full schemes developed by Le Corbusier,
Hoesli and Aujame in the first few days of the design process.[13]

already intended not only as glare protection for the clinic's north-facing, glazed front but also as an exterior boundary for the outdoor terrace-garden above.

In the following days Hoesli and Aujame took over the design process and tried several alternatives to Le Corbusier's initial scheme (see FIG 16). In that process some key elements of the project were modified and adjusted, and others, such as the *baldaquin* over the terrace (an important component of the finished project), were suggested for the first time. Compositionally, the scheme was divided into three bays, with the ramp occupying the narrower and central bay; the staircase to the residence was aligned with the ramp and occupied a central position against the back boundary wall and flanked by two open shafts. The clinic and maid's room conformed to an L-shaped plan on the first floor that partially embraced the ramp on the eastern side, while the volume of the house behind formed a perfect cube. The square, open shaft that separated clinic from house was placed against the western boundary wall and provided much needed "respiration" for the whole. In short, after one week of hard work, Le Corbusier and his two young collaborators were ready to test and develop the project at a larger and more detailed scale.

At this point, Hoesli concentrated on detailed studies of dimensioning the functional components of the clinic level, including furniture arrangement and circulation patterns. These studies were based on the initial scheme, in which the ramp was placed in the center of the site and led to a frontal volume composed of three bays. The doctor's exam room and related waiting room occupied the central and western bays, while the maid's room and its adjacent bathroom were placed in the eastern bay, exactly above the garage. This bay protruded deeper into the site, partially flanking the ramp. As expected, a brise-soleil protected this frontal volume's northern glazed façade, and a structural system of pilotis confirmed and reinforced the three-bay composition.

There are no preserved drawings available of the development of the residential portion. However, although the organization of the clinic seemed to be workable, it is apparent that some critical problems emerged in the design of the residence, especially the ramp-vestibule-stairs sequence. Therefore, on February 16, Le Corbusier tried an important modification: he removed the ramp from the center bay and placed it against the western wall, eliminating the alignment of the ramp with the staircase, which remained in the center bay at the back of the site. He placed a vestibule and a short stair perpendicular to the ramp and the staircase in the space thus generated at the southwestern corner of the site. This combination of platform + steps negotiated the half-floor difference between the intermediate landing of the ramp and the origin of the staircase to the house.

However, the problem was not yet solved. The next day, Le Corbusier moved the ramp to the opposite wall and retested the whole scheme at a smaller scale. The following week Hoesli and Aujame prepared a full set of measured drawings at 1:50 scale. In this new set of drawings several important components were finally fixed in place, while other new elements and issues began to emerge:

- on the ground floor, which maintained a three-bay composition, the ramp was definitively placed next to the eastern wall; the garage was located against the opposite wall toward the front, and the entrance to the house from the ramp's landing was located at the back of the plot
- the clinic occupied the entire front on the first floor, and the maid's rooms conformed to a rectangular volume added to the rear side of Dr. Curutchet's consultation room; both were accessible from a semi-enclosed gallery. The residential volume was definitively a nine-meter square (29.53 ft) in plan, supported by nine pilotis;[14] this cubic volume remained separated from the rear boundary wall by the staircase and by two open shafts that provided natural light and ventilation to the southern side of the house (FIGS 17, 18, and 19 opposite)
- the first level of the house, the piano nobile, was divided into four quadrants, identifiable by their furnishings as kitchen, music, living, and dining rooms; small terraces opening from the living and dining rooms at the two ends of the northern wall provided access to the roof garden located above the clinic; these two terraces flanked the largest open shaft and negotiated the transition from the two-bay organization of the residence to the three-bay composition of the clinic (FIG 18)
- the second floor of the home showed three rooms: the master bedroom opening over one part of the living room below, and two other rooms pushed to the sides of the lot; the two bathrooms were defined by curvilinear walls which "floated" within the structural grid, and provided a functional separation of the three rooms (FIG 19)
- the street elevation was dominated by a concrete brise-soleil which protected the northern wall of the clinic and extended to the terrace above

THE DESIGN PROCESS

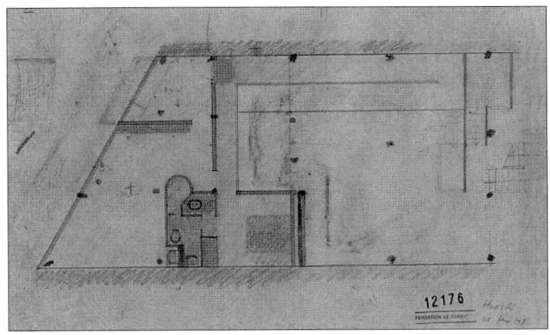

FIG 17. Plan of the clinic level, February 21, 1949. (FLC 12176)

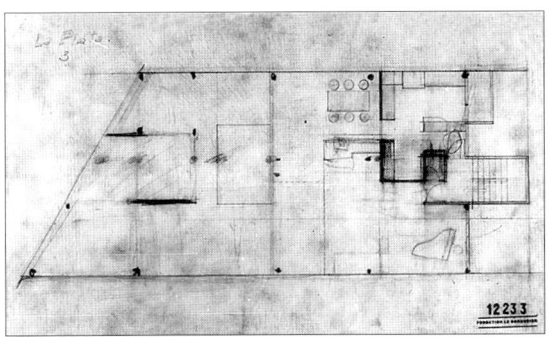

FIG 18. Plan of the lower level of the residence, mid-February 1949. (FLC 12233)

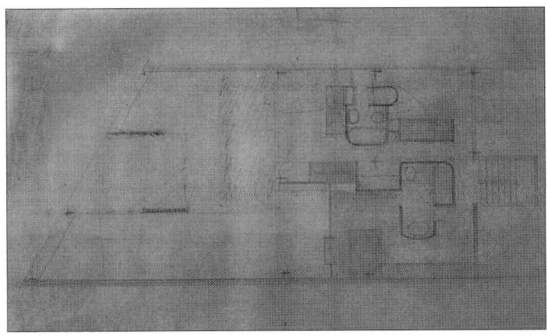

FIG 19. Plan of the upper level of the residence, mid-February 1949. (FLC 12182)

FIG 20. Elevation and perspective sketch of the street façade, February 21, 1949. (FLC 12153)

to provide both an exterior boundary and visual framing for the terrace; a small balcony protruding outward from the clinic's waiting room and aligned with the ramp, marked the entrance to the building (FIG 20, see especially the perspective sketch in the upper-right corner); the elevation was topped by a sheltered space spanning the whole width of the plot, resembling a solution similar to that adopted at Maison Cook.

The project had reached a crucial point, a functional and spatial maturity only three weeks into the design phase. The team was now ready to develop some aspects in greater detail, such as the calculations for the brise-soleils, the proportional system of the façades, the unfolding of the promenade architecturale, and the structural system of pilotis (particularly the transition from the three-bay system of the clinic to the two-bay system of the residence). This was the most critical problem and it demanded several studies and important decisions. At the same time detailed attention was given to the design of the ramp, particularly to the point of transition where the intermediate landing met the vestibule box and the stairs it enclosed. Furthermore, the bedroom level became a serious problem that demanded time-consuming and meticulous studies, a veritable "patient search," at various scales.

Regulating Lines: Modulor, Brise-Soleils and the Framed Entryway
Regulating lines had been a compositional strategy in Le Corbusier's work since the beginning of his career. In the early 1920s he dedicated a full essay to this subject, which was originally published in *L'Esprit Nouveau*, and later became a chapter in *Vers une Architecture*. For him, regulating lines were "an assurance against capriciousness, a means of verification to ratify work created in a fervour," and "a satisfaction of spiritual order [leading] to the pursuit of ingenious and harmonious relations."[15] His interest in regulating lines, the golden section, human dimensions, and particularly his wish to find and establish rules of universal application, led to a long search which culminated in the 1940s with the development of his "proportional grid according to human dimensions," later termed the "Modulor." Related to the golden section and to the human figure, the Modulor became an inseparable component of Le Corbusier's projects from the time of its conception. As William Curtis has expressed, the Modulor was more than a compositional or proportional tool; "it was a philosophical emblem of Le Corbusier's commitment to discovering an architectural order equivalent to that in natural creation."[16]

The Modulor was first implemented in large building complexes such as the Unité d'Habitation in Marseilles (1947), the Duval factory in Saint Dié (1947), and the project for the vacation complex on the Côte d'Azur known as Roq et Rob (1949), all of them contemporary with Maison Curutchet.[17] Le Corbusier was eager to test this proportional system in a single-family house, which would be more at a human scale than the large complexes in which he had already implemented it. Thus, the implications of this "proportional grid according to human dimensions" became an important aspect of the entire project. A series of annotations and calculations of the distance between floors according to Modulor dimensions appeared already in the earliest conserved drawing of Maison Curutchet's design (FIG 15). Considered essential components of the project, these dimensions governed and dictated all measurements and distances throughout the design process. Later, Le Corbusier demanded that Curutchet pursue authorization from local authorities to permit building the house according to Modulor dimensions, which, as expected, were at odds with local building regulations.

Regulating lines were also a valuable tool for the composition and design of elevations, most significantly the configuration of the brise-soleils. These elements of sun control, which like the implementation of the Modulor, became a signature item of Le Corbusier's postwar architectural vocabulary, reveal in Maison Curutchet the proportional system of the façades' composition. In late February Hoesli produced detailed brise-soleil studies in plan and section of what were considered the two most critical surfaces exposed to the incidence of the sun: the northern façades of the clinic and the residence[18] (FIG 21). Expectedly, due to their slightly differing orientations, direct sunlight affected them differently and demanded separate studies for each.

After studying the brise-soleils, Hoesli turned his attention to the design of the entire façade. In one of these drawings (FIG 22) the compositional theme of the frontal elevation was clearly established through a musical analogy: "the three melodies." These melodies (the pilotis, pan-de-verres, and brise-soleils) were identified as three independent systems which, successively overlapping one in front of the other, produced a layered yet permeable, complex plane. While the distance and size of the pilotis depended on structural need, the composition of the brise-soleils and of the pan-de-verres were determined by Modulor dimensions and by a proportional system dictated by regulating lines. These initial façade studies were contemporaneous with developments in the plan that structured the pilotis in a three-bay system for

THE DESIGN PROCESS

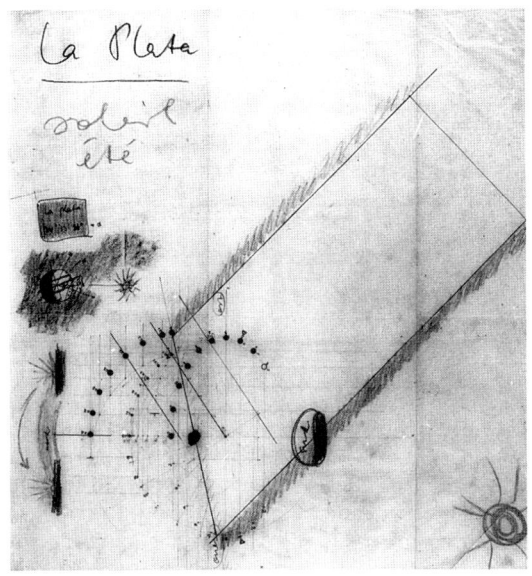

FIG 21. Hoesli's study of summer sun incidence for the development of the brise-soleils, February 23, 1949. (FLC 12140)

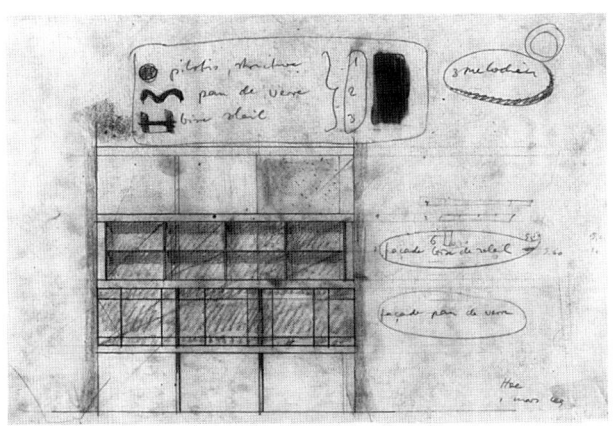

FIG 22. "The Three Melodies," drawn by Hoesli on March 1, 1949. (FLC 12151)

the frontal volume. The pilotis suggested a certain centrality, whereas the four-bay partitioning of the brise-soleil challenged that centrality and added compositional tension. Between these two elements, the pan-de-verre was subjected neither to the three-bay nor to the four-bay composition, but to a less structured rhythm, establishing a different "melody" or a counterpoint to the other two melodies. The whole frontal façade was then crowned by a horizontal plane that spanned the width of the site and was supported by pilotis rising behind the brise-soleil and the pan-de-verre. This horizontal plane, a roof covering the terrace-garden accessible from the living areas, defined a perfect square resembling the composition of Maison Cook's façade.

While the façade was being investigated, a more fundamental compositional problem—the transition from the three-bay system of the clinic to the two-bay system of the residence—still remained. On March 9, Le Corbusier finally settled this problem. He took the floor plan of the living areas and confirmed the two-bay symmetrical system defined by three equidistant pilotis (one exactly on the center line of the site, and the other two slightly detached from the boundary walls); he then extended the two-bay system into the volume of the clinic at the front of the site. The residence remained square in plan, supported by nine columns; the central column at the front was taken as a fixed point to define another square structural module that designated the depth of the frontal volume, leaving a transitional module, off the square grid, that defined the depth of the open shaft separating the clinic from the residence (FIG 23). The exact placement of pilotis was a fundamental step in defining the structural and compositional organization of the whole, and thus settled the project at 1:50 scale.

Due to this compositional change, the façades Hoesli had designed were then revised two weeks later, once the floor plans had been reworked according to the modified structural system. On March 22, Le Corbusier himself sketched out the almost definite frontal façade, adapting Hoesli's studies from previous weeks to the new conditions imposed by the two-bay structural system. Two new important elements were also introduced at this time: a concrete-framed entry way marking the pedestrian entrance to the building, and a detachment of the brise-soleil from the sides, emphasizing the façade's square plane (FIG 24). Thus, the concrete grid of the brise-soleil appeared to "float" within the virtual boundaries of the square plane defined by the ground, boundary walls and terrace roof. The introduction of the framed entryway on the left side of the façade broke the balance of the eleva-

THE DESIGN PROCESS

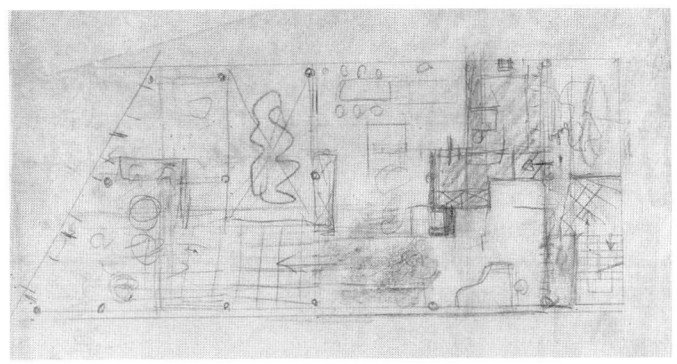

FIG 23. Plan of the lower level of the residence, drawn by Le Corbusier on March 9, 1949 (FLC 12167). Compare with FIG 18.

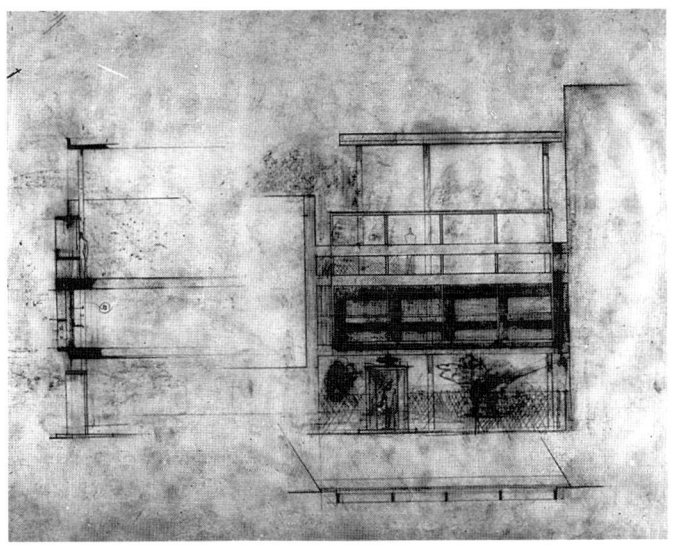

FIG 24. Street façade and section through the frontal pan-de-verre, brise-soleil, framed entryway, and baldaquin, March 22, 1949 (FLC 12150).

tion, which until then had been visually dominated by the two-bay organization of pilotis and the four-bay grid of the brise-soleil. Then, Le Corbusier shortened the span of the terrace roof so that it no longer ran the full width of the site, but was restricted to the western side, forming what he termed a "*baldaquin,*" a partial roof structure supported by four pilotis. This move established a diagonal tension between the concrete doorway on the lower left side of the plane, and the baldaquin on the upper right side. This calculated tension cut through the layered components of the façade (the three melodies) and restored compositional balance.

The baldaquin's dominant verticality not only established a compositional counterpoint to the planar frontality of the brise-soleil, and the doorway diagonally below, but also gave scale to the space. Without this partial roof, the façade would have been dominated by the high blank wall of the neighboring building. Thus, when observed from the outside, this baldaquin served to focus the point of attention toward the center of the composition and the volume of the residence behind. Moreover, this baldaquin helped to insert the building into the urban character of the street by providing the appropriate transition of scale from the massive building on the western side, to the smaller and more articulated eastern neighbor.

The design of the frontal plane established the compositional system that was to be followed in the design of the other elevations of the building. The brise-soleil of the clinic was repeated almost identically for the frontal elevation of the residence behind it, disregarding the differences of their orientations (Hoesli's studies had concluded that the slightly different incidence of the sun would not affect the design of the brise-soleils). While the southern façades did not require brise-soleils because they were not exposed to direct sunlight, the compositional rules remained the same, especially for the design of the pan-de-verres, which were encased between the horizontal and vertical elements of the exposed concrete frame. This concrete frame thus performed on the southern elevations a subdued version of the "melody" that the brise-soleils played on the northern façades.

April 1949: Le Corbusier's Final Project
The design of Maison Curutchet posed several difficulties that demanded long and careful studies before arriving at a satisfactory architectural solution, one that would fulfill the needs of the client and the goals of the architect. While neither the clinic nor the living areas presented problems to the design

team, two more difficult aspects to resolve were the vertical circulation sequence (ramp + stairs) and the bedroom level. The first had been an extremely difficult problem from the beginning. The position of the ramp within the site and the location of the stairs within the house were changed several times before arriving at a solution that appeared to satisfy the needs of the project. The stairs in particular were continually displaced and rotated until finally fixed in a seemingly appropriate position, where they remained for the rest of the design phase.

The organization of the bedroom level proved to be the most challenging and time consuming. Dr. Curutchet had requested that the three rooms be oriented toward the front of the site in order to receive direct northern sunlight and to enjoy the view of the park through wide panoramic windows.[19] This was a difficult goal considering the tight dimensions of the site. The design team had to try several alternative and progressively more complex schemes. The basic idea for the organization of this level had been established around March 16: the boundary walls would serve as an envelope within which pilotis and thin curved walls would define differentiated functional areas. Two rooms would be located at the front and a third one opening directly to the living room below, while the bathrooms would "float" in the rear as one independent volume enclosed by curvilinear walls. Numerous studies were conducted in the following days. In them, the master bedroom and the study exchanged position, and the bathrooms were split into two different volumes. Dividing the bathrooms provided a necessary independence to the three rooms, and also generated what was likely an unintended passageway. The curvilinear walls of the bathrooms now not only provided a desired counterpoint to the rectilinear edges of the building envelope, but also guided movement through the plan. Furthermore, the combination of low and high partitions that defined the bathroom enclosures provided a perceptual enlargement to the otherwise small dimensions of the rooms to which they were connected. It was a complex but spatially rich solution that had required a patient search and unusual "finesse" in order to provide access and privacy to all rooms, without abandoning the complex spatiality sought by the architect. Le Corbusier himself explained:

> This floor, which was extremely difficult to organize, offers the exceptional advantage of receiving sunlight on the whole northern façade. One should also note the finesse necessary in organizing the furnishings of these rooms, particularly the bathrooms.[20]

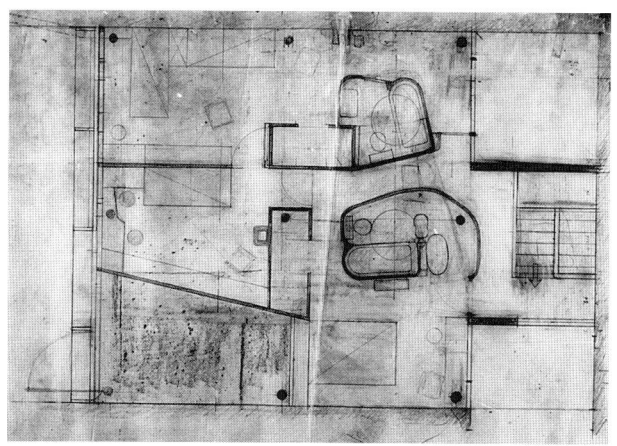

FIG 25. Plan of the (almost) final version of the upper level of the residence. (FLC 12197)

Once these more complex design problems had been resolved, Le Corbusier was confident of having achieved a sophisticated design that fulfilled his client's requests as well as his own architectural objectives. The conceptual scheme of Maison Curutchet was based on the separation of the two functional units—clinic and residence—into two differentiated volumes connected visually and physically by a ramp. The space between became a cool, interior court. Arguably, the longitudinal section was key to understanding the functional and spatial organization of the building: a carefully calculated sequence of solids and voids that simultaneously articulated the separation of the two units, while granting cohesiveness to the whole.

The site was an empty container bound by three existing walls, a readily available box that Le Corbusier had filled with a masterful display of his architectural elements and principles, in a poetic drama of space.[21] The ground level would remain virtually empty and house only areas for "traffic" (garage, pedestrian entrance, ramp), some services and vegetation. A concrete-framed doorway marked the pedestrian access on the left of the façade, while vehicular access would be to the right. Le Corbusier explained to Dr. Curutchet that the car could be left either *à l'abri* under the pilotis (that is, without the need to open the garage door) or else inside the garage, which was placed approximately five to six meters (sixteen to twenty feet) behind the property line.[22] The ramp would be the most distinct element of the ground level, defining a journey from the street up to the house at the midway landing, and then up to Dr. Curutchet's medical quarters. Adjacent to the ramp, a slightly sinuous path, meandering amidst the pilotis and proposed trees, would lead to the rear of the site, providing access to the service areas located under the vestibule of the residence.

The clinic was placed on the first floor at the front of the site, bridging its entire width. Three areas were clearly defined within it: waiting room, examining room, and maid's room.[23] Convinced that the resolution of the medical office was an appropriate and efficient response to the doctor's demands, Le Corbusier explained to his client: "It can be seen that the clinic is correctly organized for the decent reception of patients as well as to respond to the diverse functions of auscultation and examination."[24]

The residential portion, above and behind the clinic volume, formed a nearly perfect cube, also spanning the site's entire width, located to the rear of the site and suspended two levels above ground by pilotis. The lower of its two levels would house the social areas requested in the program (living room, music area, fireplace, dining room), the kitchen and a toilet. Typical of the Corbusian plan libre, the differentiated sections requested in Dr. Curutchet's brief were functionally defined by the careful placement of furniture, built-in equipment, and slab projections. The fireplace would be a floor-to-ceiling prismatic box located in the geometric center of the square plan. However, despite its central position, the fireplace was not intended to constitute a privileged point of attention. Rather, the focus would be on the relationship of the building with nature, particularly the visual relationship between living areas and the park. As one would climb the stairs from the enclosed vestibule below, and upon entering the living room, the greenery of the park would dominate the field of view. The double-story glazed, northern wall of the living room would showcase the park beyond. This double-height space of the living room was intended to further accentuate the dominant presence of the park with a similar feeling of open space. The terrace over the clinic roof could be accessed from the living room.

The kitchen and related service spaces were clearly separated from the living areas by full-height walls; it constituted a square area opening to the southeastern shaft of the site. A door provided access to an exterior balcony, which in turn would lead back to the vestibule adjacent to the stairs, supplying a service route which would avoid a trip around and through the living spaces to reach other areas of the building. This particular aspect, the need to pass through an exterior space in order to enter and exit the kitchen, may be considered a weakness of the building's functional resolution, especially considering that by merely displacing the enclosure to the outer edge of the balcony and repositioning the door, it would have been sufficient to secure an interior path from the kitchen to the rest of the building. However, Le Corbusier's decision clearly reveals two aspects of his architecture that should not be underestimated: first, the need to hierarchically and unambiguously emphasize the main path of the promenade architecturale, which could have been weakened if equally important access routes were also available from this level's vestibule; second, and probably more important, his decision to resolve the residential needs within the confinement of a pure cube, one of the Platonic forms he had praised in *Vers une Architecture*. A functionally-minded solution such as the one proposed above was not a viable one for Le Corbusier, who preferred to sacrifice functional needs to the more fundamental aspects of his architectural discourse.

THE DESIGN PROCESS

The upper floor would house, as described above, the more intimate rooms of the house. The master bedroom would be on the southwestern corner and opening directly to the double-story space of the living-room, the daughters' bedroom would occupy the entire eastern bay from front to back, and the study/guest room would be located between them, at the center of the residence's façade. The two full bathrooms would be incorporated within the privacy boundaries of the two main rooms.

Separating the volume of the residence and that of the clinic would be a large vertical open space, a fundamental element in understanding Le Corbusier's resolution of the building. Le Corbusier instructed in his drawings, model photographs, and descriptive text to plant a large tree in this area.[25] Years later, Dr. Curutchet, a physician knowledgeable about the vital needs of living organisms, admitted that he did not believe that the tree could grow adequately in that particular space, considering the amount of natural light to be insufficient. Nonetheless, he followed the architect's indication and planted a young poplar tree, observing with marvel and surprise how rapidly it grew to become a dominant element of the space in front of the house.[26]

This open shaft, the tree that grows through it, the liberated ground floor, and the terrace would constitute the building's "respiratory system." Not only would they provide an optimum separation between working and living areas, but also they would represent an extension of the park into the confines of the site, inviting the outside in. In effect, all living and working spaces were organized around these open spaces, the void space and the growing tree serving as a metaphor for that which—through a complex and clearly articulated mechanism—provides life.

Satisfied with the project's resolution, in early April the team began developing a final set of drawings documenting the entire project to send to Dr. Curutchet. These were composed of two series of drawings at two different scales.[27] A highly developed exterior perspective of the house as seen from the park was also included. These drawings were extremely precise and clear, and did not include room dimensions or notes about materials. They were pristine representations of the spatial disposition of the rooms and their architectural sequence, emphasizing the signature Corbusian elements—pilotis, brise-soleils, pan-de-verres, hanging garden, and so forth. However, the drawings did include furniture lay-outs and in some cases the design of fixed furnishings, for example the wooden cabinet separating the waiting room from the exam room in Dr. Curutchet's clinic. An accompanying eight-page docu-

MAISON CURUTCHET

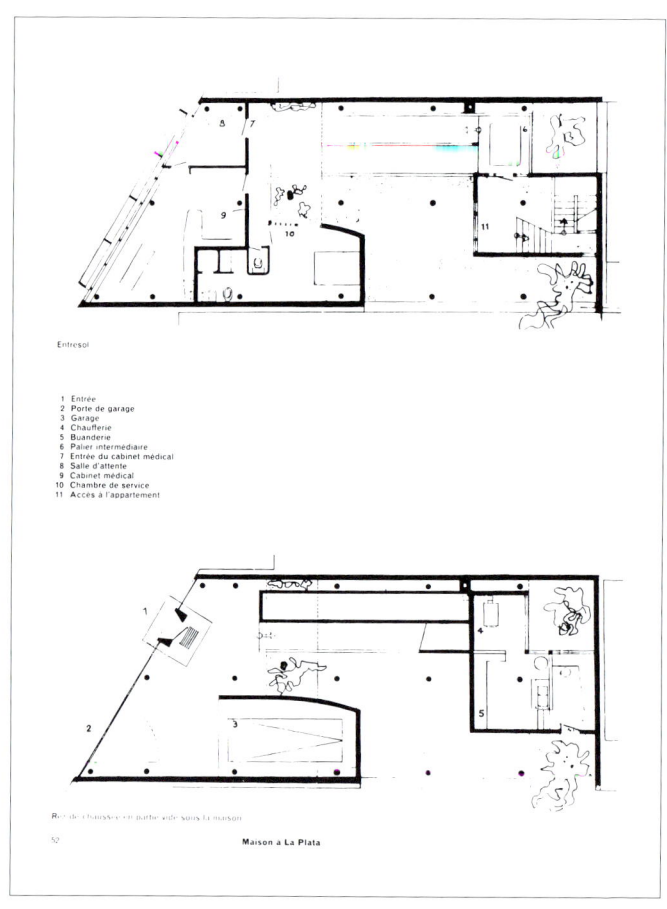

FIG 26. Plans of the ground floor and clinic volume,
as published in the *Oeuvre Complète*.

THE DESIGN PROCESS

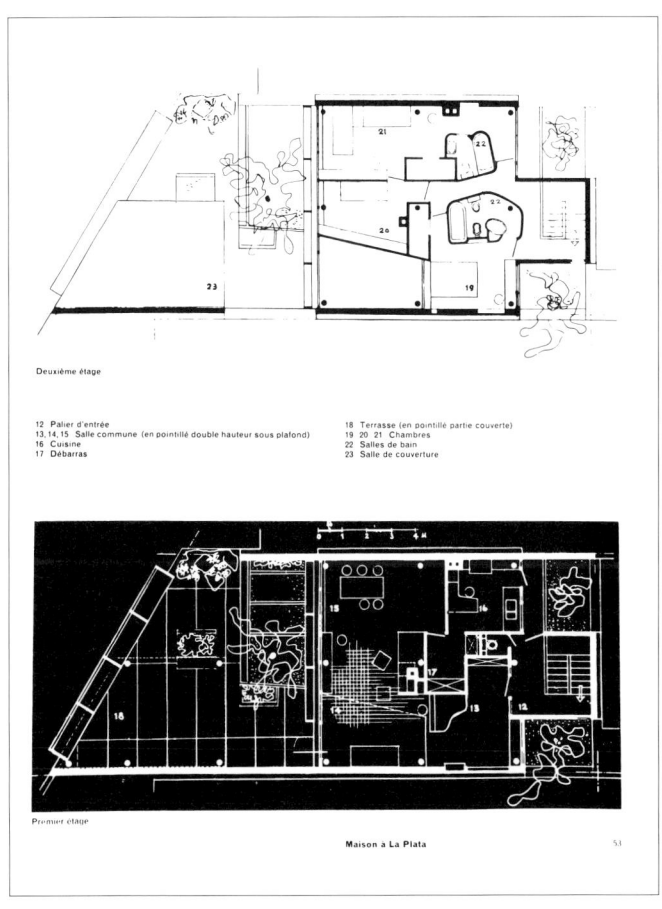

FIG 27. Plans of upper and lower levels of the residential volume, as published in the *Oeuvre Complète*.

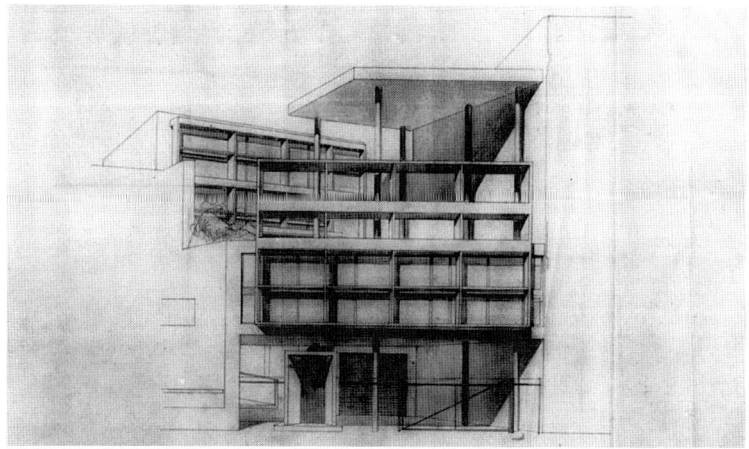

FIG 28. Exterior perspective from the final set of design drawings, April 1949. (FLC 12111: CUR 4107)

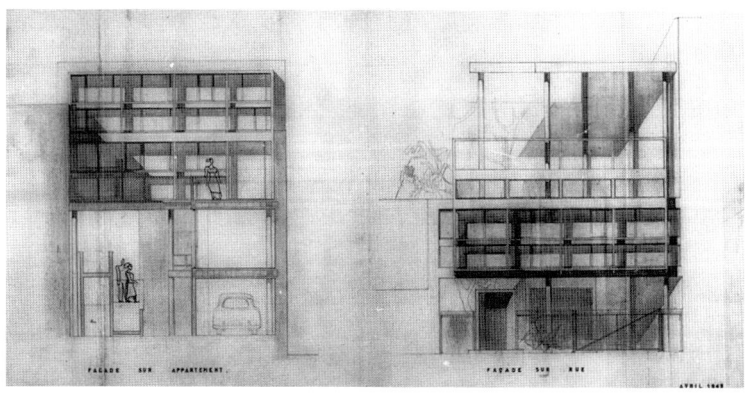

FIG 29. Façade of the residence (left) and the street façade (right), from the final set of design drawings, April 1949. (FLC 12110: CUR 4106)

ment described the textural characteristics of the spaces, materials and finishes.[28] The exterior perspective drawing emphasized the most important aspect of the design, the promenade architecturale, by placing the vanishing point at the point of penetration into the building.

The team also built a highly detailed model of the entire building at 1:50 scale. This maquette was very different from the smaller clay models that had been built at the beginning of the design process, for it served not only to test the final project in a convincing three-dimensional form, but also to provide the client and his site architect with a series of photographs to better understand the complexities of the project. Thus, Le Corbusier ordered a full set of photographs taken from different vantage points, including a bird's-eye view, and frontal and sectional views (achieved by removing the rear and side walls). The result was a convincing demonstration of the spatial qualities of his design, and above all, of the longitudinal transparency and openness of the entire composition. Furthermore, as was typical of Le Corbusier, the photographs were altered in the atelier using drafting, montage and transfer-paper techniques to further emphasize particular aspects of the project. Undoubtedly, the most interesting photographs are those showing the building's relationship to its built and natural contexts. However, interestingly, these altered photographs remained in the atelier and were neither sent to Curutchet, nor included later in the publication of the project in the *Oeuvre Complète*.[29]

Finally, on April 26, Le Corbusier communicated to his client that the set of drawings and the model of his house were complete.[30] Two days later he wrote to his friend Pablo Curatella-Manés, then an Argentine diplomat in Paris, to send the drawings and photographs of the model by diplomatic pouch to avoid delays and the loss of the important documentation of the project he had just finished.[31] After his disappointment with the Plan de Buenos Aires, and the complications with the payment of his professional fee, he had learned the frustrations involved with Argentina's bureaucratic institutions. On June 3, 1949, Le Corbusier sent the important documentation to Curatella-Manés, including the two sets of drawings, twelve unaltered photographs of the model, and one of him holding the model in front of the mural he had painted in the atelier. The accompanying document, dated May 24, 1949, described the project thoroughly and ended with a remarkably clear summary:

FIG 30. Maison Curutchet, photographic collage of the model, April 1949.

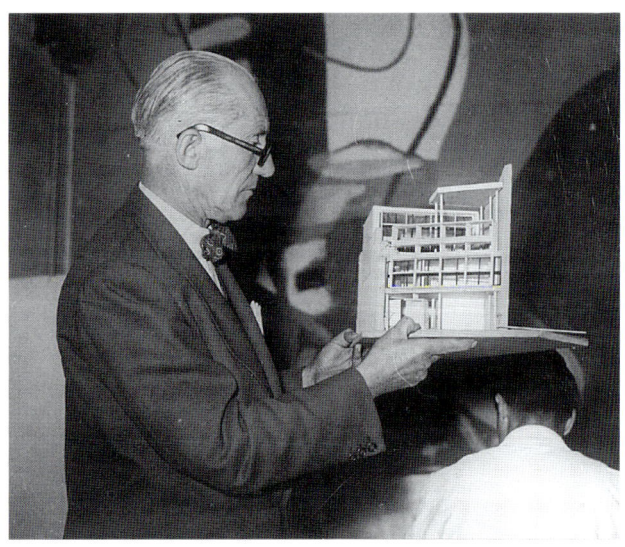

FIG 31. Le Corbusier observing the model in his atelier in Paris.

THE DESIGN PROCESS

Very constructive architecture, well coordinated in its arrangements; the volumes and the colors will add themselves to the park's landscape which will always be present with the tree, the bushes and flowers that are planned in the project. I will finish by telling you that this work has been done with extreme care and I hope that it will please you. I think that you will give it to your local architect. I have mentioned to you the names of the architects capable of assuming the supervision of this work in my letter of September 28, 1948. Of course, I remain at your disposal to make any modification that you wish. However, I would add that these modifications could not be more than small ones, for I strongly consider that I have occupied your plot with the most useful answer to your program and resources possible, as well as to the limitations of your site.[32]

In Argentina, Dr. Curutchet received the project with immense pleasure, and immediately wrote back to Le Corbusier with an exceptional response:

The elegance and transparency of the building's organization, the form and disposition of bathrooms and bedrooms, the ramps, and the overall harmonic continuity, particularly between the living room and the terrace-garden were the unexpected great news. However, after that first impression, I look and, in every detail, I find a new interest, a new mirror of clear intellectual beauty. From now on, I know that I will live a new life, and, in the future, I hope that I will fully assimilate the artistic substance of the architectural jewel that you have created.[33]

Dr. Curutchet submitted the package to Amancio Williams, whom he had selected for construction supervision. Williams began the bureaucratic process of obtaining construction permits, and soon after designated his own "Curutchet team" within his taller. In June, 1949, Le Corbusier had seemingly concluded his involvement with the design of Maison Curutchet. Dr. Curutchet in Lobería and Amancio Williams in Buenos Aires were extremely enthusiastic and looked forward to constructing the house.

Late Modifications, Working Drawings and Details
In mid-August, 1949, Williams visited the site accompanied by his "Curutchet team." He had great respect for Le Corbusier and considered his project "a spatial symphony."[34] Nevertheless, he did not hesitate to

advance a criticism about the vestibule box leading to the residence, which in his view was not resolved to the same level as the rest of the project. He wrote to Le Corbusier:

> I consider that this part is not at the same high level of resolution as the rest of the house and it will be too bad to leave it as it is; it seems to me that you have obtained this solution to avoid complications; clearly the steps "*à le petit hôtel*" added to the staircase are not in accordance with the freedom of your plan and the site is too small for a different solution. The prism is a good solution and connects well to the ramp, and it gives a sense of intimacy to the entrance of the residence, but
>> it destroys the spatial symphony of that part of the building;
>> it produces a strangulation with the garage/services volume;
>> it will be terribly dark inside that volume;
>> it provides a poor ceiling for the rooms housed beneath (heating equipment, etc.).

Williams was referring to the first flight of steps leading to the stairway, which considerably invaded the vestibule, and to the closeness, darkness and lack of transparency of this volume. In fact, the first flight of steps did look like an appendage, a last minute compromise to negotiate the different floor elevations. The vestibule, with its enclosed stairs, represented an odd object within a clear, yet sophisticated, unfolding of space. Williams, who was by then an experienced architect, studied an alternative solution to improve the "obscure aspects" of this area.

He proposed to replace virtually all of the vestibule walls (except the rear boundary wall and partially one side) with a transparent enclosure, and to completely remove the first flight of steps. The latter modification forced a 180-degree rotation of the whole staircase and required a reaccommodation of the landings at every level. Williams acknowledged that in his solution the relationship of the entrance to the ramp was not fully resolved, and most importantly, that it had not been designed according to Modulor dimensions.[35] However, his proposal did liberate the vestibule from its crowded and dark condition. Williams forwarded it to Le Corbusier for its consideration and asked him to respond or further improve it within the following twenty days; otherwise he would maintain the stairs of the original drawings.[36]

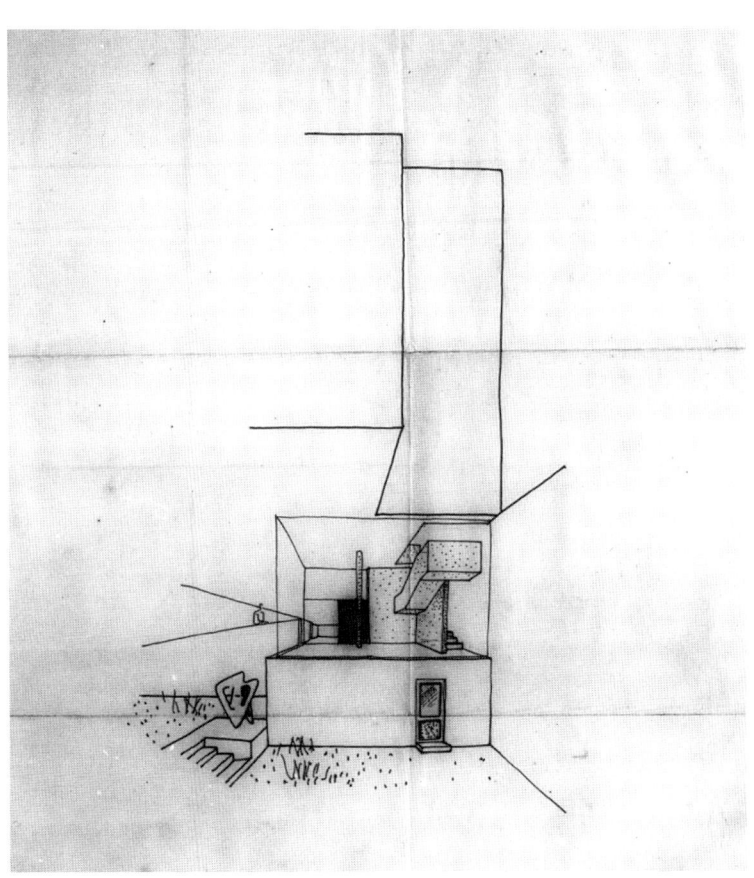

FIG 32. Williams' revised version of the vestibule. (Drawing by Williams, FLC 12142)

MAISON CURUTCHET

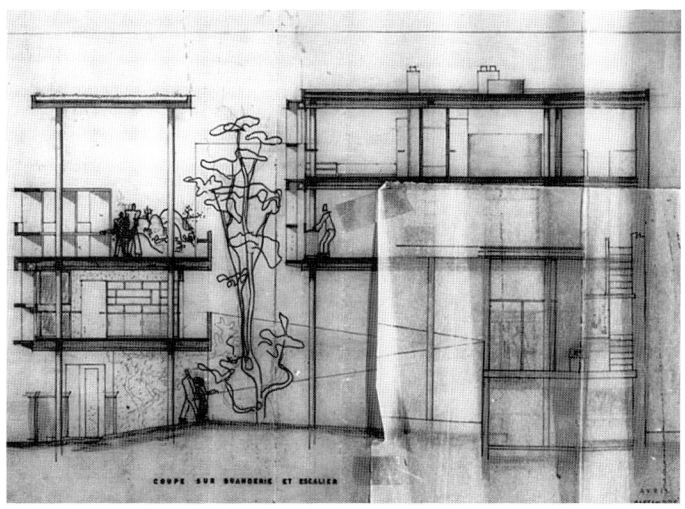

FIG 33. The longitudinal section from the set of design drawings developed in April 1949, with the correction of the stairs affixed on top, and dated September 1949. (FLC 12103. CUR 4099)

THE DESIGN PROCESS

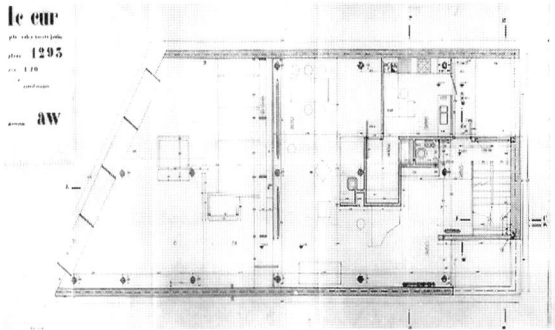

FIG 34. Plan of the lower level of the residence, from the set of working drawings developed at Williams' office. Note that the wall separating the stair area from the rest of the living spaces has been eliminated. (FLC 12118)

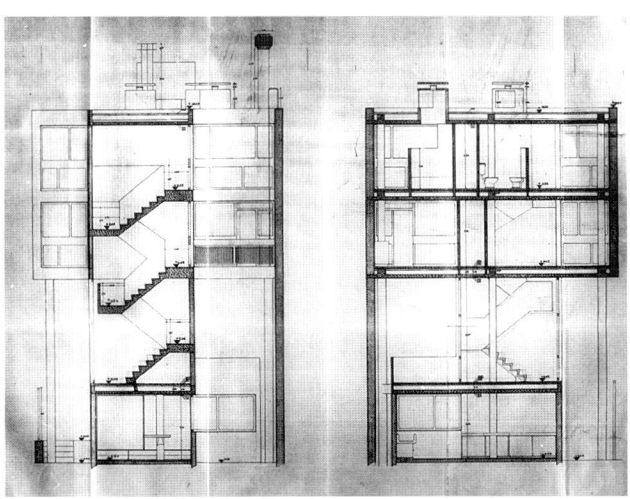

FIG 35. Cross sections of the residence, from Williams' set of working drawings. (FLC 12123)

Le Corbusier accepted Williams' critique very well: "Your criticism of the entrance to Maison Curutchet is perfectly motivated and your solution is excellent," he wrote in response.[37] The sole improvement he suggested was to remove the wall separating the two flights of steps which Williams had indicated in perspective but not in the plans he proposed. This thin wall concealed the initial flight of steps and thus flattened the perceptual depth of the vestibule. Le Corbusier's variant allowed the rear wall of the house to act as a backdrop upon which the stair was easily read as a light, delicate object. He acknowledged that this alternative presented a problem for children who could fall from the rail-less stairs, and left its resolution to Williams. Despite being a relatively small change, the spatial implications of Williams' modification to the stairs were quite significant, for the staircase is located at a crucial point in the spatial sequence of the building—the critical point of bifurcation of the promenade architecturale, the transition between exterior and interior, and the beginning of vertical movement through the residence.

Shortly after visiting the site, Williams' team started producing construction documents and developing details. Throughout the documentation, Williams remained absolutely loyal to Le Corbusier's original project, registering only very slight dimensional adjustments, particularly in the diameter of pilotis, which were slightly larger than in Le Corbusier's drawings.[38] The construction documents and details developed at Williams' office were remarkably clear, and remained a valuable and reliable source of information for the construction and eventual completion of Maison Curutchet, even after a conflict with the client determined Williams' replacement as construction supervisor.[39] Thus, through his working drawings and details, Williams left in Maison Curutchet the mark of his high professional standards, meticulousness, experience, and commitment to modern architecture.

NOTES

1   Le Corbusier signed *The Modulor* on 25 November 1948; Le Corbusier, *The Modulor 1* (Cambridge: Harvard Architecture Press, 1980), 225. *The Poem of the Right Angle* was drawn, written and calligraphied between 1947 and 1953; Le Corbusier, *The Modulor 2* (Cambridge: Harvard Architecture Press, 1980), 156.
2   Jerzy Soltan, "Working with Le Corbusier," in vol. 17 of *The Le Corbusier Archive*, ix-xxiv.
3   Le Corbusier to Aujame, 2 February 1949, Dossier Correspondence Le Corbusier (FLC G3-13): 72. Roger Aujame was then a young architect, educated at the Ecole de Beaux Arts in Paris. He had met Le Corbusier in Vézelay in 1940, and joined the atelier a few years later when Le Corbusier

THE DESIGN PROCESS

returned to Paris after the German occupation. Aujame worked on several projects including the Modulor, the Unité d'Habitation, and Saint Dié. Roger Aujame, conversation with the author, La Fondation Le Corbusier, Paris, 11 January 1993.
4   Bernard Hoesli worked with Le Corbusier for a short period. His participation in the design process of Maison Curutchet was in fact his most significant contribution to the atelier. A few years later he went to the United States and became one of the most important members of "The Texas Rangers," the group of young faculty (Colin Rowe, Robert Slutzky, John Hejduk and others) that marked an era at the University of Texas at Austin. He later became Dean of the ETH in Zurich.
5   Aujame, conversation with the author, La Fondation Le Corbusier, Paris; 11 January, 1993. For a description of this process of design-through-models, see Jerzy Soltan, "Working with Le Corbusier," xiv.
6   Aujame, conversation with the author, La Fondation Le Corbusier, Paris; 11 January, 1993.
7   Le Corbusier to Curutchet, 7 February 1949, Dossier Villa du Dr. Curutchet (FLC 12-07A): 64.
8   Ibid., 31.
9   See for example Curtis, *Le Corbusie: Ideas and Forms*.
10 Soltan, "Working with Le Corbusier," xv.
11 Ibid., xiv-xv
12 Aujame, conversation with the author, La Fondation Le Corbusier, Paris, 11 January, 1993. Although these clay models have not survived, through the drawings and studies preserved at the Fondation Le Corbusier, it is possible to reconstruct to some extent the volumetric and functional search developed in the early stages of the design process.
13 I have attributed the design scheme at the far right to Aujame, although it was not signed. Aujame did not regularly sign his drawings, but both Le Corbusier and Hoesli did. The lines of these drawings have a different quality than those signed by either Le Corbusier or Hoesli, and it is a safe assupmtion, since Aujame was the only other person working on the project, that the drawings are his. Also, on the lower right side of these drawings there appears what could be an "A."
14 One similar, yet undated floor plan of the living areas (FLC 12187) showed a system of pilotis for the house repeating the three-bay composition for the front volume.
15 Le Corbusier, *Vers une Architecture*. From the English translation of the 13th. French edition, *Towards a New Architecture* (New York: Dover Publications, 1986), 75.
16 Curtis, *Le Corbusier, Ideas and Forms*, 164.
17 In fact, the manuscript of *Modulor 1* was finished on 25 November 1948, during the period that passed between the acceptance of Curutchet's commission and the actual beginning of its design phase.
18 It should be noted that in the southern hemisphere, and especially south of the Tropic of Capricorn, the north façade is the principle sun exposure.
19 "Exposición Sumaria," 33-49.
20 "*Cet étage extrêmement difficile à organiser offre cet avantage exceptionel de prendre son soleil sur la totalité de la façade nord. On remarquera également la finesse qui était nécessaire pour organiser l'ameublement de ces pièces dans de bonnes conditions, les installations sanitaires en particulier.*" Le Corbusier to Curutchet, 24 May 1949, The Curutchet Collection.
21 In fact, as Stanislaus von Moos has noted, the idea of the box and the container is one of the themes that Le Corbusier explored throughout his career. von Moos, *Le Corbusier: Elements of a*

81

Synthesis, see especially Chapter 3 "Typology and Design Method," 69-141.
22 Le Corbusier to Curutchet, 24 May 1949, The Curutchet Collection, third page.
23 In Le Corbusier's original project the rooms for the maid were located on this level. However, in the finished building, the maid was assigned rooms on the ground level under the vestibule. The areas in the first floor that were originally designed for the maid were to be used instead by an eventual nurse, or as a recovery room. However, these spaces never performed either of the two functions, remaining underutilized. Alcira del Carmen Curutchet de Goggi, daughter of Dr. Curutchet, to the author, Buenos Aires, April 1994.
24 Le Corbusier to Curutchet, 24 May 1949, The Curutchet Collection, fourth page.
25 "*Un arbre aura pû être planté au niveau 1 dans la vide réservé devant la façade de l'appartement; ses feuillages pourront monter à volonté.*" Ibid.
26 Casoy, "Entrevista," 8.
27 The first set of drawings, Serie I, 1:50 (at scale 2 cm/meter), included a full set of floor plans (rez-de-chaussé, levels 2, 3, and 4 CUR 4094-97), a concrete structural framing plan (CUR 4098), three longitudinal sections (CUR 4099-101), four cross sections (CUR 4102-105), and two façades ("clinique" and "appartement," CUR 4106). The second set, Serie II, 1:20 (at scale 5 cm/meter), was composed of three floor plans (levels 2, 3 and 4, CUR 4108-10), and a more detailed longitudinal section (CUR 4111). The perspective drawing inserted between them was labeled CUR 4107.
28 Le Corbusier to Curutchet, 24 May 1949, The Curutchet Collection.
29 This omission is most likely because despite the interesting characteristics of these photomontages, the quality was either inferior to that of the unaltered photographs, or because the montages were meant as tests only, and not for further review.
30 Le Corbusier to Curutchet, 26 April 1949, The Curutchet Collection.
31 Le Corbusier to Curatella-Manés, 28 April 1949, Dossier Villa du Dr. Curutchet (FLC 12 07 A): 66.
32 "*Architecture très constructive, très coordonnée dans ses aménagements; ce sont les volumes et les couleurs qui s'ajouteront au paysage du parc qui sera toujours présent avec les avant-plans d'arbres et d'arbustes, et de fleurs qui sont prévues au plan. Je terminerai en vous disant que ce travail a été fait avec un soin extrême et je veux espérer—et je souhaite—qu'il vous donnera satisfaction. Je pense que vous allez le communiquer à votre architecte local. Je vous avais indiqué sur ma lettre du 28 Septembre 1948 les architectes capables de prendre en charge la surveillance de ces travaux. Il est bien entendu que je demeure à votre disposition pour apporter toutes les modifications qui vous sembleraient désirables. J'ajouterai, toutefois, que celles-ci ne devraient être que des modifications de détail car j'ai le sentiment très net d'avoir occupé votre terrain le plus utilement possible pour répondre à votre programme et aux ressources, aussi bien qu'aux défauts de ce terrain.*" Le Corbusier to Curutchet, Paris, 24 May 1949, The Curutchet Collection, sixth and seventh pages.
33 "*La estructura grácil y transparente del edificio, la forma y disposición de los baños y dormitorios, las rampas, y la armoniosa continuidad en todo y en particular entre el salón y la terraza jardín fueron la primicia. Pero después de esa primera impresión, miro y en cada detalle, descubro un nuevo interés, un nuevo espejo de diáfana belleza intelectual. Desde ahora comprendo que viviré una nueva vida, y más adelante espero asimilar plenamente la substancia artística de esta joya arquitectónica que Usted ha creado.*" Curutchet to Le Corbusier, 12 June 1949, Dossier Villa du Dr. Curutchet (FLC 12 07 A): 70.
34 This and the following quote from the letter Williams to Le Corbusier, 14 September 1949, Dossier Amancio Williams (FLC R3 07 A): 216.
35 Ibid., 217.

36 Ibid.
37 Le Corbusier to Amancio Williams, 22 September 1949, Dossier Correspondence Le Corbusier (FLC G3 14): 50.
38 Another interesting aspect of this phase was Williams' enthusiasm over the Modulor. He asked Le Corbusier to send him as much information and material as he could to implement the system as faithfully as possible (Williams to Le Corbusier, 14 September 1949). Le Corbusier replied by sending a "*tirage de la règle papier du Modulor*" 2.26 meters long, and instructed Williams on how to use it, and to keep it in his pocket inside a small Kodak film container (Le Corbusier to Williams, 22 September 1949). Williams' enthusiasm was demonstrated by his persistence in using Modulor dimensions at all costs, becoming very upset every time he found obstacles to the experiment ("Lepera Report," informal annotations taken by Luis and Julio Grossman during the renovation of the house in 1986-88).
39 The complete set of working drawings produced at Williams' office consisted of nineteen sheets that included all four floor plans, a roof plan, three sections, and elevations of windows and doors (all at 5 cm/m scale). The rest of the drawings were of specific details for windows, doors, and the fireplace; kitchen cabinets and counters; closets and built-in furniture; handrails, fence, skylight and other metallic and hardware details; and various concrete details (particularly the stairway to the residence and the slab over the garage). Curiously, Williams' set of drawings did not include elevations of the façades.

Architecture is a work of art, a phenomenon of the emotions, lying outside questions of construction and beyond them. . . . The purpose of architecture is to move us. . . . Architecture is a matter of "harmonies," it is a "pure creation of the spirit."

—Le Corbusier, *Towards a New Architecture*, 19

CHAPTER III

BUILDING MAISON CURUTCHET

Once Dr. Curutchet had selected Williams, and before Le Corbusier had begun the design, Curutchet met with Williams at the architect's house in El Tigre sometime in the first half of October 1948, and engaged his services as construction supervisor. Williams was very interested in the project and agreed to do the job without charging professional fees. He wrote to Le Corbusier on October 21:

> I received Mr. Curutchet's visit, whom you have addressed to me. I thank you for your confidence. . . . I told him that for the supervision of construction of your project, I will only ask him to pay for the expenses that it originates, but not for my professional honorarium.[1]

Despite the fact that the design process of Maison Curutchet had not yet started, and that information about the site eventually became necessary, Williams was not involved in any part of the project until the design work was completed and Dr. Curutchet had received the drawings from Le Corbusier. When Dr. Curutchet needed professional services that could have been provided by an architect—for instance a rendition of the characteristics of neighboring buildings—he did not seek Williams' help but instead requested it from his young friend, E. Alberto Ringuelet, who was a land surveyor and engineering student.[2]

Williams reappeared on the scene once the design was finished, and Dr. Curutchet had sent him copies of the drawings he had received from Le Corbusier. Apart from producing working drawings and directing construction, Williams assumed the responsibility of obtaining legal permits for two very important aspects of the work: first, the authorization to disregard the regulations imposed by La Plata's building code in favor of Le Corbusier's Modulor dimensions; and second, the official recognition of Le Corbusier as the author of the work. As Williams himself pointed out, the first was very important for the realization of the work, the second was a matter of principle, an issue of professional respect beyond legal boundaries.[3] These two issues were very important for Williams, and seemed to be his conditions for accepting the job. Unexpectedly, the procurement of a construction permit did not present problems. The Municipality of La Plata recognized the work to be of "scientific interest," and allowed its construction to override building code stipulations.[4] Conversely, however, recognition of the European architect as author of the work was a much more bureaucratic procedure and presented problems that proved to be unsolvable.

At that time, Argentinean law prohibited someone who was not registered as a professional architect in the country to be listed as author or director of construction in official permits and documents. Amancio Williams presented an interesting argument: Le Corbusier as author and Williams as director of construction. This would mean that within current legislation, he assumed legal responsibility for the construction of the building, whereas Le Corbusier would remain as author, the signature artist. Williams also argued that Le Corbusier's name could be used because he was an honorary member of the Academia Nacional de Bellas Artes, Argentina's art association.[5] On October 1, 1949, Williams wrote to his friend Alberto Prebisch, an architect from Buenos Aires who had met Le Corbusier in 1929, and to Alberto Falomir, president of the professional architects council, to obtain their support. Three days later he sent a letter to the president of the professional engineering council of the Province of Buenos Aires, Hector Daneri, formalizing his request.[6] In reply, Mr. Daneri requested a letter or other documentation that clearly established that Le Corbusier had asked Williams to undertake this responsibility.[7]

Initially, the council decided to grant permission to use Le Corbusier's name as author of the work.[8] However, it appears this decision was premature, for nearly one month later, a member of the council complained, demanding that standard legislation be observed and that Le Corbusier's name not be included anywhere as performing any professional service, including design. As a result, the council reversed its previous decision and denied authorization to use Le Corbusier's name in any way.[9] In spite of this setback, and of his former commitment to take charge of construction only if Le Corbusier's name were respected, Williams decided to continue as director of construction.

In October, 1949, Williams sent Curutchet a contract, establishing the scope of his services, expecting the client to sign the document that would determine their mutual obligations. By this time, however, Curutchet was getting anxious and discouraged because of the unexpected length of the process and because of the growing inflation rate in Argentina. He replied to Williams on November 5, 1949:

> I received the contract. . . . When I asked Le Corbusier to design my house, I had the funds to build it and a little extra money that left me with a comfortable budget. Today, that capital is just enough to build one-half of the house. . . . For the time being, I decline to sign the contract. If the situation is not defined soon, I even consider the sacrilege of abandoning Le Corbusier's beautiful project, and later having a new design of easier construction, something that could be done by someone from La Plata. . . .[10]

In addition to these growing financial concerns, the relationship between Amancio Williams and Pedro Curutchet was becoming slightly strained. The argument between them was centered on the selection of a general contractor. While Dr. Curutchet considered a local contractor from La Plata to be more convenient from a financial point of view, Williams insisted that only a contractor from Buenos Aires could carry out a project of such caliber. Having very strong opinions about who should be in charge of building a house designed by Le Corbusier, the architect defended his position with tenacity. He replied to Dr. Curutchet with a seven-point letter arguing that the cost of Le Corbusier's project was lower than one of average quality designed by a local architect, and that much had already been spent, and would be lost by abandoning the project at that point. He also insisted that a local contractor would not reduce construction costs. Moreover, Williams urged Curutchet not to forget the efforts of the many people already involved and argued that the house should be built both for the benefit of Dr. Curutchet and for the sake of architecture. Finally, he reminded his client that because he had withdrawn his professional honorarium, he had no personal financial interest in the work. The letter concluded with a proposal consisting of two points that he submitted for Curutchet's consideration. First, he would personally work on a plan to lower the cost of construction by changing materials without altering the spatial characteristics and quality of the project. Second, he mentioned that he had recently spoken with the owner of a construction company in Buenos Aires who had agreed to start the building with a down payment of 200,000 to 250,000 pesos (approximately 22,400 to 28,000 dollars), and that the rest could be financed through a loan.[11]

At that point in the process Williams' argument prevailed: in late November, 1949, Dr. Curutchet made a down payment of 223,000 pesos (approximately 25,000 dollars) to Petersen, Tiele and Cruz, the construction company Williams had selected.[12] The contracting company began the production phase of technical and legal documents necessary before actual construction could start. Simultaneously, Mr. Petersen tried to obtain a construction loan for Dr. Curutchet at the Banco Hipotecario. Unfortunately, however, by the end of the year the process of procuring a loan was becoming more and more complex. The Banco Hipotecario was a highly bureaucratic federal financial institution that demanded additional drawings, permits, and other documentation in order to extend the loan. Furthermore, the proximity of the holiday season, the beginning of Argentina's summer and the long distances that separated the many people involved in the operation slowed the decision-making process.[13] In February, Williams and Dr. Curutchet exchanged letters regarding these frustrations.[14] The client was increasingly worried and discouraged by the slow advancement of the process, which, combined with the rising inflation rate, continued to consume his already diminishing funds. In the meantime Argentina's financial situation was getting worse: rising interest rates made it extremely difficult to procure loans on reasonable terms. It was soon clear that it would be impossible to secure a loan to finance the remaining cost of construction. Thus, Petersen, Tiele and Cruz preferred to cancel the contract, and returned most of the down payment. They retained 17,000 pesos (1,900 dollars at that time) for the work completed thus far, which had included the procurement of municipal documents, the structural calculations, and initial foundation work.[15]

After the contract with Petersen, Tiele and Cruz was rescinded, Dr. Curutchet, extremely frustrated, decided to halt construction. He again considered abandoning the project. Once more, however, the determination of Amancio Williams became the deciding factor to continue. On March 3, 1950, he sent a letter to Dr. Curutchet outlining his position and opinions about the events that had culminated in the cancellation of the construction contract.[16] Williams also described the work produced at his own office to lower construction costs, and the increasing difficulties he encountered in working with subcontractors, especially to obtain estimates for various aspects of the work. In the last paragraph of the four-page letter he urged Curutchet to reconsider his decision of abandoning the project:

> After all the effort made this work cannot be abandoned. The difficulties are enormous, but the will of men is extraordinary and overcomes everything that depends on them. To abandon this work is to commit suicide[.] I earnestly ask you, Curutchet, to work together. . . . Do not forget that things are resolved for good only with an extraordinary tenacity.[17]

Dr. Curutchet was again persuaded by the architect. On March 11 he informed Williams of his decision to continue the work.[18] Although the loan had not been approved, he instructed Williams to proceed as if it had been. He explained to him that he expected to receive help, if necessary, from friends and family to finish building the house. Dr. Curutchet also acknowledged and expressed gratitude to Williams for his extra work and energy accorded to this project despite the fact that he had declined a professional fee, but insisted that the architect be paid for his services.[19] It was apparent that Dr. Curutchet had developed a sense of obligation toward Williams simply because the architect had declined an honorarium. Thus, Curutchet attempted to establish a more standard professional relationship between himself and the architect. However, Williams again declined any payments beyond the expenses the project would generate in his *taller* (mostly employees' salaries and supplies). He also updated his client on the manufacturing and construction status of certain pieces of furniture that were being custom built for the house.[20] Two months later, in May, 1950, Williams reported to Le Corbusier that construction was about to begin. He added that it was "a victory over the instability and inflation that have become terrible here."[21] He also communicated to Le Corbusier that the professional council of the Province of Buenos Aires had denied authorization to utilize Le Corbusier's name as the author; and therefore the house would be built under Williams' name.[22]

Thus, by the end of 1950 Williams had twice persuaded Curutchet to build the house, prepared all working drawings and technical calculations, and ordered custom pieces of furniture. Most importantly, Dr. Curutchet had renewed his interest in the building, despite the long and unexpected sequence of problems that he had had to overcome from the very beginning of the process two years earlier.

The Building Process Part I: Williams and Ringuelet
As it can be appreciated in the few buildings built by Amancio Williams, he was an extremely meticulous architect. In Maison Curutchet, he was perhaps even more so, likely because it was a project designed by Le Corbusier, whom he recognized as his master, and sought to complete the project with the highest possible quality. Maison Curutchet's structure of reinforced concrete should in theory have presented no major challenges to the local construction industry in Argentina, where reinforced concrete is typical of an outstanding number of well-known buildings built both previous to and contemporaneous with Maison Curutchet. However, Williams' standards for a project designed by Le Corbusier demanded that he import special concrete machinery, and thus he had sought a contracting company capable of providing the most up-to-date techniques.[23]

In order to persuade Curutchet not to abandon the project, however, Williams was now willing to negotiate what he had not accepted before: the selection of local contractors. Dr. Curutchet asked his young friend E. Alberto Ringuelet (who was already involved in some aspects of construction administration) to find a local construction company to continue building the house. Ringuelet had already assisted Dr. Curutchet in 1949 by procuring information and producing drawings on the site's existing condition. Later, when construction of the house began, he became a personal advisor to Dr. Curutchet. Upon Curutchet's request he succeeded in finding local contractors for the bulk of the work. Three independent professional engineers based in La Plata became the contractors: David Tessler, concrete structure; Fidel Malisse, electrical; and A. Tilloux, plumbing systems.[24]

In early 1951 construction had resumed, and by early July of that year the concrete slab of the first floor was poured. Once again, Dr. Curutchet had renewed enthusiasm for the house and hoped—probably misled by the inexperienced opinion of Ringuelet—that it could be completed in nine months, that is, by the end of March, 1952. In late July, 1951, after two years of silence, he reported the status of the project to Le Corbusier and included some recent construction photographs. One of the photographs showed the "construction team": Ringuelet, Tessler, Martín and Malisse, posing with Dr. Curutchet. The absence of Amancio Williams or anybody from his office markedly demonstrated Curutchet's deteriorating relationship with Williams. In spite of his prior statement of gratitude toward Williams for his efforts to complete the building, Curutchet, worn out by the argument over

FIG 36. Maison Curutchet under construction. Photograph taken on July 4, 1951, and sent to Le Corbusier later that month.

FIG 37. "The construction team," from left to right: E. Ringuelet, F. Malisse, D. Tessler, S. Martín, Dr. Curutchet.

the selection of a construction company and growing unexpected expenses, was losing his initial confidence in the architect.

In fact, Dr. Curutchet avoided contact with Williams as much as he could. Shortly after construction had resumed, he asked his daughter Alcira del Carmen to become his liaison to Williams.[25] As expected, communication between the two became more and more difficult. Their differences surfaced again in the selection of furniture for the house. Dr. Curutchet wanted modern furniture and had initially asked Williams to advise him regarding furniture selection. The architect had recommended the purchase of twelve units of a chair designed by César Janello, an Argentinean architect and designer, who had recently fabricated fifty units. He also mentioned that it was possible to import original Le Corbusier furniture at reasonable costs through Curatella-Manés, the Argentinean sculptor and diplomat friend of both Williams and Le Corbusier.[26] Dr. Curutchet wrote to Le Corbusier on July 30, 1951, requesting drawings of the architect's furniture designs to have them custom built in Argentina under the supervision of his daughter Alcira.[27] However, neither Williams nor Curutchet's requests concerning furniture ever received an answer from Paris.[28]

In spite of the friction and lack of communication with his client, Williams was still the official construction supervisor, which entailed administrative and legal responsibilities, and the production and supervision of construction documents. His role was often in conflict with the interests of Ringuelet, who had gained control of the situation in the midst of the conflicts between Williams and Curutchet. Although Ringuelet's "official role" was still that of advisor to Dr. Curutchet, he was also interested in being hired as a painting subcontractor, in association with the electrical contractor Fidel Malisse. Williams strongly opposed this selection, arguing that the team lacked experience. Moreover, he had his own ideas: he was studying the possibility of using a special wall-plastering process called *enduído apomizado*, which, in his opinion, only a few, large and experienced contractors from Buenos Aires could apply successfully.[29] He also claimed that he was awaiting instructions from Le Corbusier on the color selections for the house because "the author of a work creates the harmony of forms and colors under light."[30]

While the painting issue remained unsettled, the relationship between Amancio Williams and Dr. Pedro Curutchet continued to deteriorate. Their shared objective of achieving completion of the house had taken two clearly different and often opposing paths. For Williams, the house was a masterpiece of architecture; quality of construction and fidelity to the original spatial richness of the project were his prime objectives, even if a slow construction pace, experimentation and higher, although not entirely unreasonable, expenses were necessary. On the other hand, Dr. Curutchet wanted to finish his house as soon as possible without sacrificing quality standards, but at the lowest possible cost.

In September, 1951 the relationship finally exploded. Dr. Curutchet wrote to Williams complaining about several issues, including paint, furniture design, construction problems and unexpected expenses. The letter ended with an ultimatum: to continue, he wanted a firm commitment from Williams to achieve completion by the end of March 1952; otherwise, he would dispense with his services as director of construction.[31] Williams answered promptly, claiming that much of the problem was the involvement of Ringuelet who was inexperienced. Moreover, citing Ringuelet's intentions to be hired as subcontractor, Williams pointed out the obvious conflict of interest as well as Ringuelet's possible mismanagement of procedures and purchase of equipment. Finally, he refused to guarantee completion by the date stipulated by Dr. Curutchet, arguing that it was not only against all previous agreements between them, but to guarantee such an unrealistic completion date would be professionally irresponsible.[32] He demanded, should Dr. Curutchet disagree with his response, three actions from the client:

- a letter of cancellation of the contract, including a note of thanks to the architect for his services without charge, as well as a complete description of the status of construction to-date.
- a letter to the Mayor of La Plata (with a copy to Williams) explaining his decision and expressing thanks for Williams' professional services.
- a decision concerning the chairs by Janello that had already been ordered.

The letter ended with his regrets for the three people affected by the sequence of unfortunate events: Le Corbusier, the author of the design; Dr. Curutchet, the client who, in Williams' own words "had had the courage to commission and build a high quality house"; and himself, the site architect, who had worked very hard to see this house built with no interest in compensation.

That same day, September 21, 1951, concrete had been poured into the framework of the top slab. The reinforced concrete structure, excluding the brise-soleils, was complete. Dr. Curutchet did not respond to Williams' requests, and proceeded to rescind the contract, thus ending Amancio Williams' three-year involvement with Maison Curutchet. In those three years he had not only persuaded Dr. Curutchet several times to continue with the project, but also left a valuable set of construction drawings. If it weren't for his participation, persistence and respect for Le Corbusier' original project, the house would likely have suffered major modifications, and may not have been built at all. Therefore, it is fair to say that to a great extent, Amancio Williams is responsible for the physical existence of the house, a significant role that far exceeded his professional responsibilities and participation as the first construction supervisor of Maison Curutchet.

The Building Process Part II: Ungar and Ringuelet
After ending the relationship with Williams, Dr. Curutchet asked Ringuelet to look for a new construction supervisor, demanding that the architect selected be committed to finishing the house and be accessible to discuss issues with him. He specifically recommended that this architect should not be someone from Le Corbusier's original list of four (Kurchan & Ferrari Hardoy, Antonio Bonet, Gomez Gavazzo, Williams).[33] At that point, Dr. Curutchet still had unlimited confidence in Ringuelet, despite the accusations raised by Williams during the final days of their professional relationship. Ringuelet selected Simón Ungar, an experienced architect based in Buenos Aires, who had also maintained a tangential relationship with Le Corbusier in the 1940s, through direction of an Argentinean journal.[34] Due to his unlimited respect for Le Corbusier and for the project itself, Williams quite graciously facilitated the transition by providing Ungar with a full set of drawings (Le Corbusier's and his own) as well as construction specifications.

As Ungar took charge, he imposed a new rhythm of construction, expecting to complete the project by the end of June 1952. The brise-soleils, most masonry work, and the electrical and heating systems were finished within his first four months as supervisor.[35] He also reported to Le Corbusier the project's status, mentioning that he had been forced to introduce modifications in bedrooms and bathrooms and in some details; however, he claimed that these changes had been made while conserving the essence of his design. The most significant alterations were in the bathrooms and in the spatial relationship of the bedrooms to the living room's double-story space. Ungar never consulted his client about making these changes. This later upset Dr.

Curutchet immensely, who considered it a sacrilegious violation of Le Corbusier's magnificent creation. Despite the initial push, however, construction slowed down again in mid-1952, and one year later the house was still unfinished. On October 26, 1953, Ungar's representative at the construction site, a Mr. Mangano, visited Le Corbusier at his atelier in Paris.[36] Mangano's mission was to obtain color specifications for painting the house, which was nearing completion. Le Corbusier quickly sketched the floor plans of his project and specified color tones for walls, columns, niches, doors, windows, and other elements of the building. Although he had received Ungar's letter concerning modifications to the project, he had not been informed of the nature of these modifications, and thus his floor plans no longer represented the actual building.

Shortly after, however, the unlimited confidence that the client had shown toward Ringuelet, and the high esteem he had developed for Ungar, transformed into serious accusations of deceitful administration, leading to the expulsion of Ringuelet and two of his collaborators from the site. Dr. Curutchet also considered dismissing Ungar, but seeing that a lawsuit with the architect could potentially halt construction for three years, the doctor found it appropriate to carefully avoid such a situation.[37]

In addition to financial problems and disputes with the site architects, Dr. Curutchet also faced unexpected technical problems that emerged during the construction process. The concrete structure had been completed impeccably by Tessler, but technical problems arose in other parts of the job. The masonry work was deficient in some areas, particularly lintels, causing leaks that affected plaster and paint finishes. The asphalt membrane of the terrace failed three times, plumbing leaks abounded, the floor of carob-wood tiles had to be laid twice, and the columns were mistakenly given a smooth finish with white cement, instead of exposed concrete, as Williams had proposed.[38] Nevertheless, and despite all these problems, by the end of 1953 the house was almost complete and was ready for the finishing touches. Dr. Curutchet judged then that the presence of a construction supervisor was no longer important and, since his problems with Ungar had not yet been settled, he decided to end the architect's involvement at that time. He personally prohibited Ungar to access the construction site. He hired a professional engineer, a Mr. Valdez, to administer the final stage of construction.

Completion and Final Details
In December, 1953, Le Corbusier's old friends Pablo and Germaine Curatella-Manés had the opportunity to visit the building with Curutchet's daughters. Later, they conveyed their impressions to Le Corbusier:

> . . . a lively house, and above all, space and natural light everywhere; one forgets that the plot is tiny. The living room with its adjacent terrace-garden that will be a continuation of the park, are a success; one cannot say that one lives within four walls. Conclusion: excellent artistic and functional results.[39]

The house was by then almost finished and, upon Curutchet's daughter's request, Germaine Curatella-Manés wrote to Le Corbusier concerning three issues that had to be resolved before the Curutchet family could move in. The first issue concerned the excessive sunlight at the bedroom level and in Dr. Curutchet's clinic;[40] the second point requested finishing specifications for the ramp; and the third issue concerned color specifications for painting the interior spaces, a task that had not yet been started even though Ungar had already received this information from Le Corbusier. Another aspect concerned the placement of a sculpture that had been indicated in Le Corbusier's drawings for the house.[41]

It is astonishing to see how the interior and exterior painting of the house, which would typically be considered a minor issue, became a very important theme of discussion throughout the construction process. It had already been a controversial issue almost three years earlier when Amancio Williams was in charge of construction. Simón Ungar, whose relationship with Dr. Curutchet at this point was anything but good, was still director of construction and claimed that he had a painting project from Le Corbusier himself. Obviously, he referred to Le Corbusier's sketch during Mangano's visit to the atelier only two months earlier. In spite of Ungar's affirmation, and eagerness to proceed, Dr. Curutchet had decided to engage the services of a "young abstract painter" to develop a color scheme related to Le Corbusier's architectural and painterly ideas.[42]

Le Corbusier responded to the letter promptly, providing clear specifications and sketches for all four aspects raised in her letter. The painting of the building was also Le Corbusier's primary concern. He demanded that the specifications he had given to Mangano be strictly respected: "I do not want pale and evanescent paint. I demand my vigorous colors." He

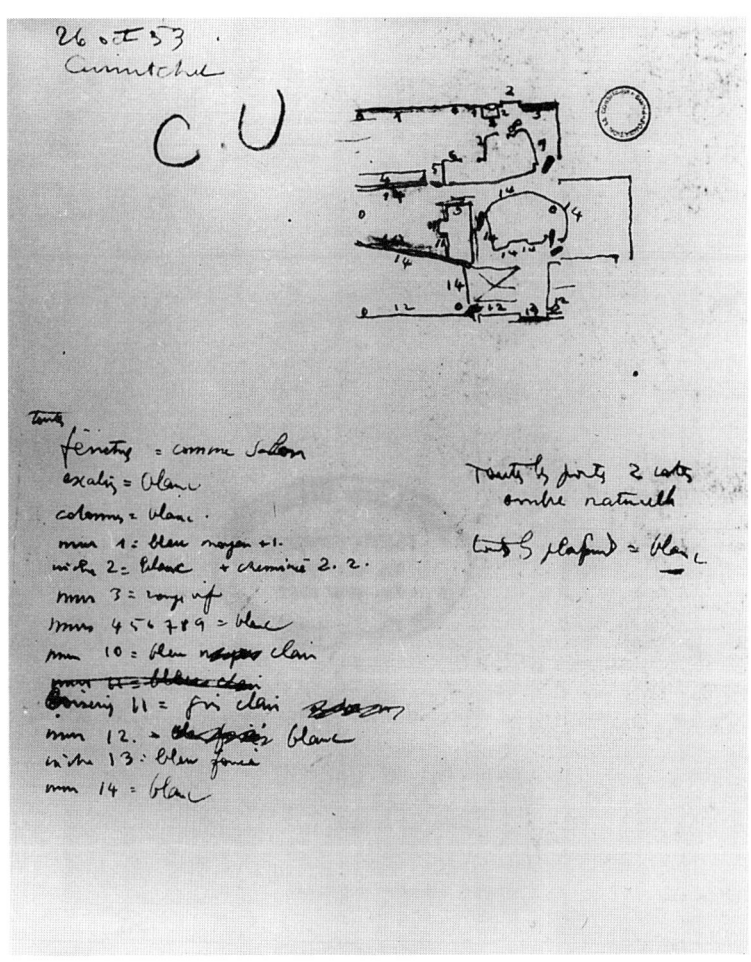

FIG 38. Le Corbusier's painting scheme for the upper level of the residence, October 26, 1953. Equally detailed instructions were also provided for the lower level.

even noted the brand of paint to use and sent its color chart, warning that if his instructions were not closely followed, "you risk catastrophic results."[43] Finally, the interior and exterior of the building were painted in 1954, but not according to Le Corbusier's instructions.[44] Years later, Dr. Curutchet claimed that he was unaware of the situation, and decided to wait until it was necessary to repaint the interior to conform to the architect's color indications.

Concerning the sculpture, Le Corbusier argued that his design was complete "*en elle-même*"; and that it was not necessary to add a sculpture to "complete his composition." He suggested that Dr. Curutchet should, if possible, include one of the admirable fossils from La Plata's neighboring museum of paleontology, or a small or medium-sized modern sculpture. In any case, the sculpture should not be considered architecture, but a piece of furniture, insisting that the sculpture not obtrude his architecture.[45] The sculpture, which Dr. Curutchet had already commissioned from Enio Iommi, was eventually placed on the ground floor between the garage wall and the cubical volume that houses the vestibule to the dwelling.[46] For the remaining two issues, excessive sunlight and flooring of the ramp, Le Corbusier provided schematic drawings of his proposed solutions. He suggested hanging curtains from horizontal bars at two different heights to regulate sunlight penetration, and proposed a concrete floor for the ramp, to be striated at regular intervals to avoid slipping.[47]

Early in 1952, just after Simón Ungar had taken over, but without Le Corbusier's involvement, Curutchet had ordered "contemporary style" custom-made furniture: china cabinets, kitchen cabinets, and shelving for the medical office, bedrooms, and vestibules were built into the walls. Many of these cabinets and closets became partitions that separated one room from another, such as, for example, the separation between the medical office and its adjacent waiting room. Also the chairs designed by Janello, which had been proposed by Amancio Williams, were acquired but not used in the dining room as planned. Some were placed in Dr. Curutchet's medical office and in other parts of the house. Finally, vegetation was planted according to Le Corbusier's drawings, despite the client's suspicion that some of the plants would not receive enough light to grow properly. In 1954, after a six-year process that had presented obstacles of all sorts, Maison Curutchet was ready to be inhabited.

FIG 39. Iommi's sculpture on the ground floor, placed in the space between the garage, the ramp, and the vestibule. The tree and some vegetation are also visible.

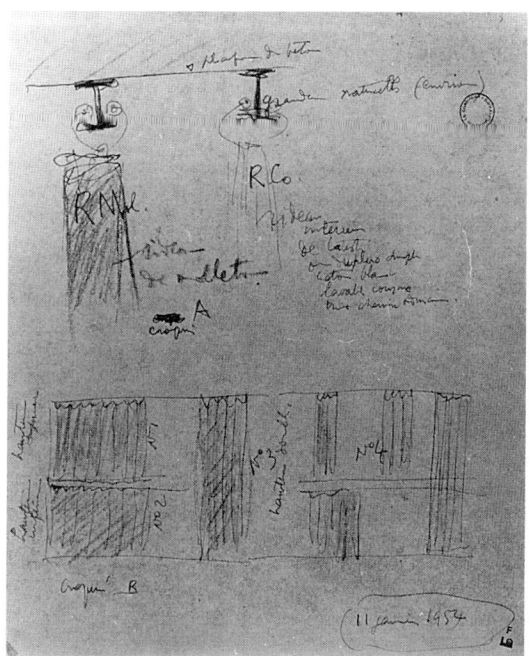

FIG 40. Le Corbusier's sketch for a system of curtains to alleviate the excessive penetration of direct sunlight, January 11, 1954.

BUILDING MAISON CURUTCHET

The Construction System, Details and Services
As Le Corbusier had mentioned in his instructions, the concrete structure *is* the building itself. The party walls provide lateral enclosure while the pan-de-verres seal the two ends of the box as defined by the concrete structure. Only a few additional masonry partitions were necessary to provide spatial definition to the different functional spaces. The system Le Corbusier had proposed consisted of cylindrical concrete columns, a small number of beams, and square concrete slabs reinforced by short-load distribution beams running perpendicular to the sides of the site. He indicated the application of a "false ceiling" attached to the underside of the short beams, which was to constitute a smooth and, for the most part, uninterrupted surface. The space generated between the distribution beams, and between the ceiling and the underside of the slab's horizontal plane, was reserved for plumbing and electrical ducts.[48] Williams eventually implemented a reversal of Le Corbusier's proposal, that is, a variation of the same idea: he placed the slab's horizontal component below and applied floor surfaces above the short masonry pillars, which were built over the concrete slab. This solution recalls the construction of the House over the Brook which Williams had built for his father only a few years before. Thus, the ceiling is no longer a false plane attached to the concrete beams, but on the contrary it is the underside of the concrete slab, plastered and finished as a smooth and continuous white plane (see FIG 41).

As had been the case in most of Le Corbusier's single family houses—and despite his own theories and hopes of universal standardization and mass production—most features of Maison Curutchet had to be custom built, especially door and window openings, built-in furniture, and cabinets. Amancio Williams undertook the detailed design of most of these items, and they bear a striking resemblance to many of the features he had used in his father's house. Several of the details reveal clever solutions to functional problems. For example, the vehicular gate to the garage, a rectangular structure, needed to swing open toward the interior of the site, yet the ground slopes upward. In order to negotiate this change in slope, Williams designed an ingenious device consisting of a counter-weight and a wheel to roll up the sloping ground plane. Another innovative detail can be seen in the bathrooms, which are heated by hot-water circulation radiators. Composed of a grid structure of pipes, the radiators were placed under the towel bar and thus also serve as towel dryers. This towel dryer, however minor a detail, stands as an emblem of the house and its modernity. Along with the solution for the vehicular

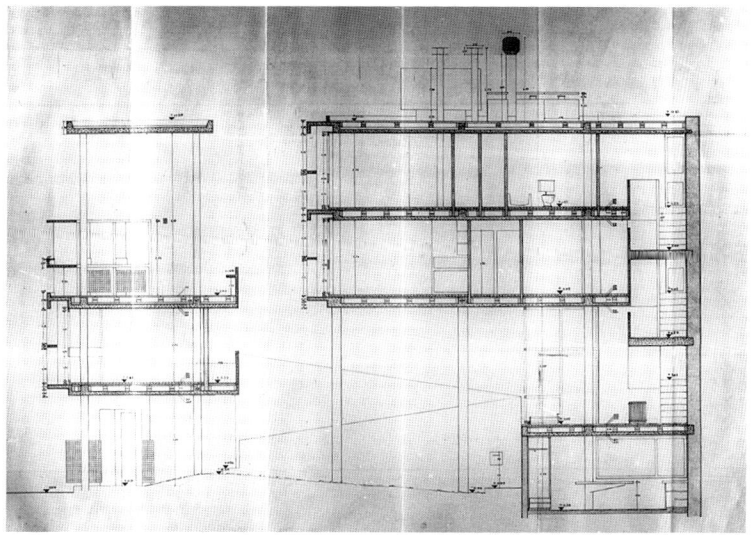

Working drawings developed at Williams' office.
Above: FIG 41. Longitudinal section; note the reversed position of the concrete slab. (FLC 12121)
Below: FIGS 42, 43. Details for manufacturing windows and pan-de-verres. (FLC 12127)

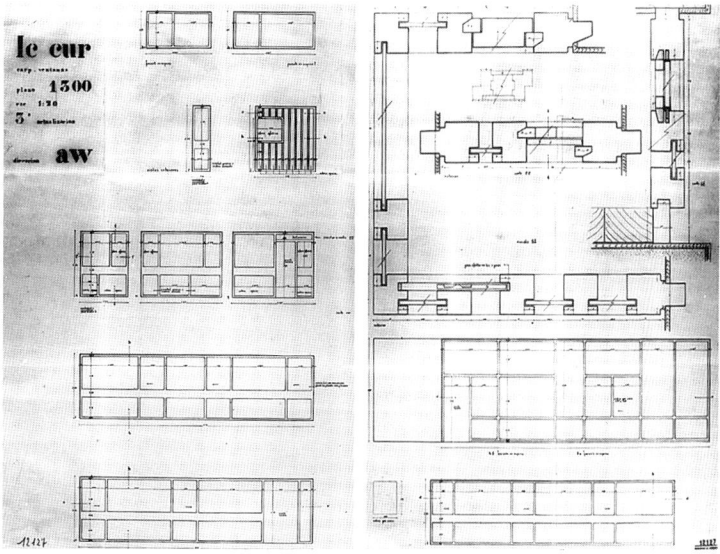

gate, the towel dryer is an "intelligent" device typical of modern architecture. Moreover, these details clearly exhibit the importance of Amancio Williams' participation in the process, for if the details and finishes are typical of modern architecture and of Le Corbusier's work in general, they are even more typical of Williams' work and his modern obsessions with appropriate sanitary living conditions, efficiency and clever resolutions.

The details for constructing the pan-de-verres were also developed at Williams' office using Le Corbusier's façades and sections as reference (FIGS 42 and 43). An examination of these working drawings and of the resolution of the structure, details and hardware of the pan-de-verres, shows again striking similarities with Williams' House over the Brook. One of the most notable and interesting examples is the resolution of operable windows: they consist of unframed glass planes which slide sideways on rails carefully cut into the fixed wooden frame. A circular brass handle is the only, quite minor, visual obstruction of the view to the landscape beyond, consistent with the building's overall visual transparency.

As suggested by Le Corbusier, all exterior walls and surfaces received a smooth stucco finish and were painted white.[49] The concrete-framed doorway that defines the main entrance to the building constitutes the only exception: it was painted with the typical grayish tone of exposed concrete. All exterior floors, including the ramp, are paved with concrete. The ramp's concrete floor is striated at regular intervals to avoid a slippery surface, and its side parapet walls are topped with a wooden handrail. All openings and metallic elements (with the exception of the black fence at the front) were painted in a medium blue tone; wooden elements (handrails and window and door frames) were varnished, polished and treated to resist their exposure to the exterior without altering their wooden appearance. Compared to the uniformly painted wooden frames of his buildings from the 1920s, the exterior finishes to the Maison Curutchet reflect Le Corbusier's change of attitude toward accepting a more natural and less machinist language.

For the building's interior walls Le Corbusier had indicated a carefully calculated color palette: white was the dominant color throughout, but bright colors (blue and red) and pale grays were chosen to highlight certain vertical surfaces of the inner enclosure as well as niches cut into the outer envelope. However, as indicated previously, the house was not painted according to Le Corbusier's specifications. Moreover, the alterations during construction changed the sequence of vertical planes, in some cases substantially. Thus, although the color palette implemented was somehow similar to Le Corbusier's, the spatial implications of these colors were different. Materials, finishes and furnishings for the interior of the clinic were carefully specified by Williams to satisfy high standards of hygiene. Walls, ceilings (rigorously at 2.26 meters, or 7.4 feet from the floor) and pilotis are painted white, while the floor is covered by a variety of irregularly shaped marble chips that create a continuous, practically jointless, polished surface. Modern and simple lighting fixtures strategically placed provide a variety of lighting alternatives for the different needs of the clinic.

Le Corbusier had initially proposed to floor the living areas with ceramic tiles, and the bedrooms with "a simple pattern of oak parquet, or with a linoleum surface or a continuous carpet, or with square ceramic tiles like in the dining room."[50] However, he either reconsidered his proposal or did not remember it, for when he later forwarded color specifications for wall surfaces he indicated that the floor should be covered with a brown wood. This latter alternative was then adopted, and the floors of all living areas and the bedrooms were covered with a pattern of small square tiles of carob-tree. Years later, Curutchet regretted that the parquet alternative was not chosen.[51]

All plumbing, gas and electrical canalizations were placed in the void channels generated between the slab's short beams and between the horizontal component of the concrete slab and the flooring system. These ducts and pipes converge in a metal vertical shaft placed against the eastern boundary wall. Heating is provided through a hot-water circulation system and coil radiators. The central boiler is placed under the ramp's second flight, efficiently located near the shaft that collects the vertical canalizations. Radiators are located at specific points throughout the building, generally next to the pan-de-verres and boundary walls.

The House as Built: Differences with the original project

As discussed at the end of the Chapter Two, the first modification to the original project (the version published in the *Oeuvre Complète*), the change of the staircase in the vestibule, was undertaken by Le Corbusier in September, 1949, following Williams' criticism of the project. The most relevant aspect of this alteration was the elimination of the initial flight of steps that invaded the vestibule, and its replacement by an additional flight of steps to the main stairs, forcing in the process a 180-degree rotation to the ascending sequence.

FIG 44. Dr. Curutchet's consultation room.

FIG 45. The living and dining rooms.

MAISON CURUTCHET

FIG 46. View back toward the ramp's midway landing and the glazed vestibule, with the stairs to the residence inside.

FIG 47. View from inside the vestibule box, at the landing of the stairs, looking toward the front of the site.

A related modification was the replacement of the fairly solid enclosure of the vestibule by a much more transparent, almost fully glazed envelope. The staircase was built as shown in the working drawings, but the vestibule's glazed envelope was again modified during the construction phase: the western side wall, which in the latest version had been shown as fully glazed at the ground floor, was built as a solid masonry wall, then plastered and painted white. The reasons, time and motivations for this alteration to the latest design version are not entirely known. However, it is possible to assume that the change was related either to structural problems in supporting the stairs, or else to compositional aspects of the side facade, particularly the junction of the stair box to the cubical volume of the house.

The revision of the ascending sequence of the staircase forced the redesign of the two side elevations of the staircase, a task undertaken by Williams himself. He reversed Le Corbusier's elevations by placing the design of the western side on the eastern facade, while slit windows were added on the eastern side providing natural light to the opposite landing (that is, he maintained the alignment of the vertical windows with the ascending movement through the stairs). Another important contemporaneous modification was the removal of the partition and door that separated the stair box from the living spaces on the first level of the residence. As far as is known (from correspondence and other documents), Williams never discussed this change with Le Corbusier or Curutchet, possibly because he assumed that it was a natural consequence of the 180-degree rotation of the stairs. As minor as it seems, however, this alteration substantially changed the spatial perception of the sequence. Whereas in Le Corbusier's version the partition would have filtered and delayed the overwhelming presence and luminosity of the park until arriving in the living room, as built, the occupant is allowed to already *see* and *feel* the presence of the park from the stair's intermediate landing.

This modification also had functional implications, because the living areas, particularly the music corner, lost some privacy due to its proximity to the main and only staircase of the house, a functional aspect that greatly annoyed Dr. Curutchet, who consider it a betrayal of the architect's conception.[52] As a result of this alteration, this small area underwent further modifications in the construction phase; the adjacent toilet was slightly enlarged to include a sink (more in accordance with Argentina's customs), and the configuration of the kitchen area was also slightly modified.

FIG 48. View of the living room from the pan-de-verre, looking back toward the stair. Note to the left the modified profile of the partition wall with respect to Le Corbusier's original project, as well as the wooden fin partition of the master bedroom above.

The combination of these two small alterations resulted in elongating the fireplace's lateral wall farther into the rear of the volume, producing a more directionally channeled space, instead of the sequence of smaller and fluid spaces envisioned in Le Corbusier's project, and an overall spatial reduction of the music corner. However, these alterations also produced a visual shielding of the service access to the kitchen and thus allowed the music corner to regain some of the intimacy it had lost with the removal of the glazed partition.

The bedroom level was the area most affected by modifications during construction, which radically changed some of the spatial and functional implications of Le Corbusier's project. Ungar introduced substantial alterations to the layout of the bathrooms and their spatial relationship to the bedrooms. As previously mentioned, in Le Corbusier's original project, the bathrooms were enclosed by a combination of curvilinear partitions of varying heights that established an intentional counterpoint to the rectilinear edges of the outer envelope, and visually and perceptually enlarged the small size of the rooms. As built under Ungar, however, this complex geometry was drastically simplified to a combination of one curved wall connected to rectilinear planes, virtually eliminating the dialectic relationship that Le Corbusier had carefully established between the hard, linear edges of boundary walls, and the soft, curved walls of the bathrooms. Moreover, the low partitions that separated sleeping areas from the bathrooms were replaced by almost full-height partitions topped by a band of transparent glass approximately 30 centimeters (12 inches) high, a vague trace of Le Corbusier's original conception. More natural light penetrates through translucent operable skylights. These changes were surely related to local privacy customs; however, they altered the spatial perception of the bedrooms, which now appeared more confined and visually smaller. The outer sides of the bathroom walls were painted white, while the interiors were fully covered by very small and inexpensive ceramic tiles.

Ungar's change to the bathrooms forced a redistribution of other components of the plan, such as closets, access to the three main rooms, and furniture layout. Nevertheless, in the built version one small space was gained without altering the physical envelope: it is a small semi-private space, a little *secrétaire*, open and related to the area of arrival to this level, which also serves as a small vestibule before entering the daughters' bedroom. However, this space was gained at the expense of eliminating the private vestibule of that

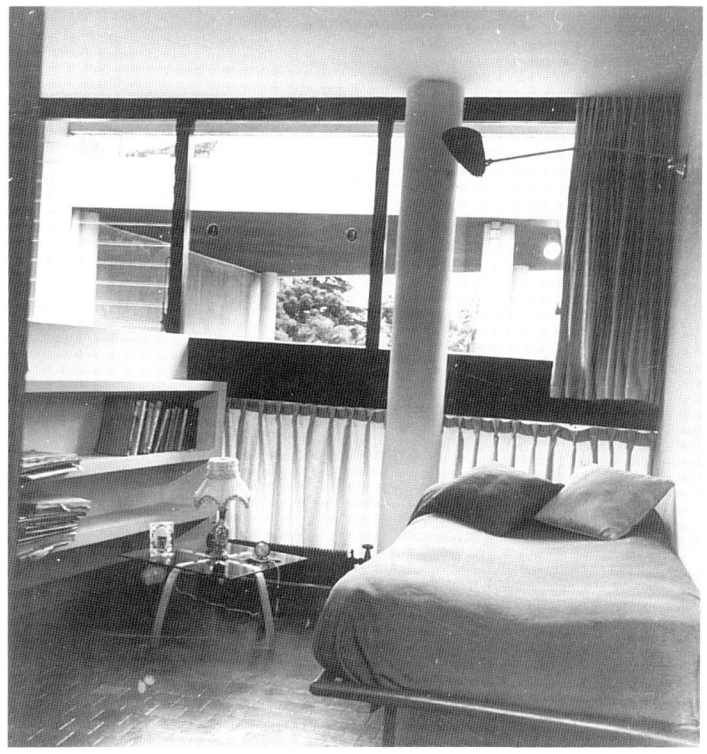
FIG 49. The study/guest room, with built-in shelves along the shortened wall at left.

room, thus reducing the size of the bedroom.

Another alteration to Le Corbusier's project, and probably the most important, was Ungar's decision to replace the full-height wall that separated the study/guest room from the double-height space over the living room by a shorter wall. The implications of this modification were manifold and greatly upset Dr. Curutchet. The most important functional implication was the resulting lack of privacy for the master bedroom, which itself was already open to the living room one floor below, and is now also visually connected across this open space to the adjacent study on the same level, due to its partial wall. In Le Corbusier's design, the open wall of the master bedroom conveyed a sense of control to the house owners, who could look down upon the open space of the living room below from their command position. With Ungar's removal of the full-height wall of the adjacent study, however, this empowered position of the master bedroom becomes one lacking privacy and acoustic isolation—nearly the opposite of Le Corbusier's intended effect.

The positive aspect of this change is that the space feels larger and even more open; above all it provides broader views to the terrace and the park beyond. Later, Dr. Curutchet had a system of pivoting wooden vertical fins installed in the master bedroom, which, extending from floor to ceiling, provided visual privacy, but only slightly improved acoustic isolation. However, on the negative side, once these vertical fins are closed, the park no longer belongs to the space, constituting a fundamental and unfortunate alteration to Le Corbusier's conception. The shorter wall of the study/guest room was also supplied with a series of three built-in concrete shelves that serve as a wide protective railing. Even though Le Corbusier had indicated a long and low piece of furniture in this position, it is unlikely that he had intended a concrete element. In fact, Williams' construction drawing did not include this built-in element at all.

In the clinic volume, the toilet and shower of the maid's room were also modified during construction. However, these small changes did not significantly alter the spatial perception or functional organization of the building as a whole. The same applies to the reorganization of the ground-floor spaces under the ramp and the vestibule, which are results of Ungar's decision to add a concrete spiral stair at the ramp's midway landing in order to access the spaces below the vestibule (the laundry room under the ramp landing, and general storage and the mechanical rooms under the second flight of the

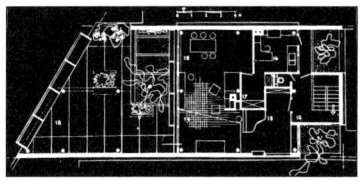 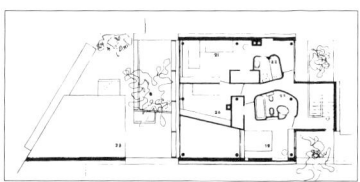

FIG 50. The original design of the residence as published in the *Oeuvre Complète*. Lower level at left; upper level at right.

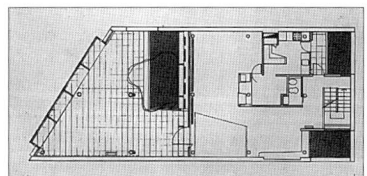 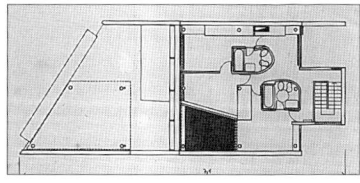

FIG 51. Floor plans of the residence as built. Lower level at left; upper level at right.

ramp). The addition of this spiral stair provides an easier, or at least shorter connection of the living areas above to the service rooms below. Although it did not affect any of the most important features of the overall composition, it represents a misunderstanding of one of the single most important aspects of the project: the unfolding of the promenade architecturale. The introduction of these stairs to the level below now offers an unintended detour, a distraction at the point of bifurcation of the vertical circulation system, the most critical moment of the promenade architecturale.

Ungar was a qualified and experienced modern architect, who had embraced the principles of rationalism as the dominant credo of modern architecture. Accordingly his modifications sought to improve the building through more rational, functional solutions. Thus, while it can be argued that most of his changes did improve the function of the building, his approach to Maison Curutchet came from a different point of view that misunderstood the subtle poetry and spatial plasticity that Le Corbusier had so carefully constructed.

Le Corbusier was not at all involved in the construction of the building, and he never saw it in person. He only knew it in its built form through the printed image—photographs sent to him years later by Dr. Curutchet, Williams and other "admirers"—and by the enthusiastic comments he received from some of his Argentinean friends. While the alterations incurred during construction did change the spatial relationship of a given room to the landscape, these modifications did not affect the overall spatial sequence, producing a built work that can truly be considered representative of the drama and spatial poetry that Le Corbusier envisioned in his original project.

Occupation, Abandonment and Rehabilitation
Maison Curutchet shares with other emblematic houses designed by Le Corbusier, such as the Villas Savoye and Stein-de Monzie, the curious status of having been inhabited by its owners for only a short time. It is certainly paradoxical that after more than six years of struggle to build the house, the Curutchet family inhabited it fully for slightly more than a decade and left it virtually abandoned until 1987 and 1988, when, under the sponsorship of Fundación Christmann, the building underwent a major rehabilitation.

By the time Dr. Curutchet's family finally moved into the house in 1954, their needs had already changed. For instance, Alcira del Carmen, one of his two daughters, was married that same year, and thus only lived in the house for a very short time. Dr. Curutchet enjoyed his house despite some problems, such as the intense light that, even after the installation of the specially designed curtains, penetrated through the pan-de-verres; he often complained that the intensity of light did not allow him to sleep well.[53] Nevertheless, he refused to install light-control devices because Le Corbusier had not specified them, showing an unusual case of client respect for the architect-designer. The only alteration he made to the building was of a functional nature: the maid's bedroom and related spaces adjacent to his medical office were, upon the occupation of the house, intended to be used as a room for a nurse.

Even before it was finished, the house became a mecca for students and professionals who wanted to see first-hand a building designed by the famous European master. Once completed, the Curutchets lived in what Alcira del Carmen called "a permanent display" for an unceasing parade of people interested in visiting the house who often did not respect the privacy of its inhabitants.[54] This situation continued to aggravate Dr. Curutchet's ambivalent relationship with his house that had begun with the difficulties he encountered in the construction process, the excessive cost, and the personal problems he had with those involved.[55] A few years later Mrs. Curutchet contracted a heart illness, and the excessive vertical circulation (ramp and stairs) necessary to move through the house became problematic.[56] Thus, in the mid-sixties Dr. Curutchet decided to move back to Lobería to continue his rural practice and dedicate more time to writing books on the surgical instruments and techniques he had created. Nevertheless, the house was not fully abandoned; he used it to stay overnight on his frequent professional trips to La Plata. Due to an almost complete lack of maintenance, however, it soon began to deteriorate. Moisture generated by water leaks and lack of ventilation affected wall and ceiling finishes (these were problematic even in the very beginning). Conversely, the reinforced concrete structure remained virtually unaffected, proof of the high quality of the work realized by the concrete contractor, and by Williams' production of construction documents.

The house remained uninhabited most of the time, although a housekeeper occupied the maid's quarters in the basement (below the vestibule), and had access to the kitchen on the second floor. This situation did not change, despite the ever more sporadic travels of Dr. Curutchet who maintained his house almost fully equipped. As late as the late 1970s Dr.

FIG 52. The building as found before the 1986-87 restoration by Luis and Julio Grossman, showing the devastating effects of years of poor maintenance.

Curutchet was still using the house on an infrequent basis. In 1978 Jorge Silvetti, professor at Harvard University Graduate School of Design, visited the house for the first time and found it in a sorry state of disrepair. He even found it difficult to photograph because of the poor state of wall and ceiling finishes.[57]

Then, in late 1986, due to the forthcoming centennial of Le Corbusier's birth, Maison Curutchet received renewed attention. As a result, Argentina's national commission on historic landmarks proposed to declare it a national historic monument, and one year later, in December 1987, this proposal was confirmed by a government decree.[58] This status prevented any damage or alteration to the house that could affect its cultural and architectural value.

Simultaneously, a project for the restoration of the house was undertaken by the Fundación Christmann, a non-profit organization for surgical research, which selected Maison Curutchet as the site of its cultural and professional activities.[59] Architects Luis and Julio Grossman, from Buenos Aires, were selected for the building's rehabilitation, which began in 1987. The project posed several challenges to the design team. On the one hand, it required substantial rehabilitation; on the other hand, the new programmatic requirements as headquarters for the Fundación, combined with its status as national monument, presented functional challenges. Nevertheless, the architects proceeded with their task, collecting as many testimonies as they could from those who had been involved in its original construction. The objective was to restore the house to its original condition, or more preferably, as close to Le Corbusier's original project as possible without altering existing conditions. Thus, for instance, the house was painted following much more closely Le Corbusier's color specifications (although still not absolutely correct).

Luis and Julio Grossman proposed only one change to the existing structure that derived directly from the building's new function. The garage was transformed into a gallery/waiting room for the Fundación Christmann; therefore, they proposed making an opening in the back wall to bring more natural light to the space and to provide it with a view of the ground floor garden, the ramp, the vestibule, and Enio Iommi's sculpture. Once the opening had been executed, however, the alteration provoked the complaints of innumerable local professionals and preservationists. Forced by the circumstances, the architects had to close the opening, replaster the wall and restore the garage to its existing condition.[60]

In June 1988, Maison Curutchet was re-inaugurated, as a national monument and the headquarters of the Fundación Christmann. For the first time the house was fully available to the general public. However, its destiny was not yet definitive. One year later, the Fundación Christmann left the house after an unsuccessful negotiation of the lease. The house was again abandoned and inhabited by housekeepers only, an elderly couple who occupied solely the maid's room and parts of the basement. Once more, the house began to deteriorate due to poor maintenance.

In January 1991, the house received a new tenant: the Colegio de Arquitectos de La Plata. The Colegio, a professional association of architects in La Plata, signed a rental contract with the Curutchet family to establish their central office, and took on the responsibility of repairing and refurbishing the house once again. Thus, in 1992, after a second restoration, the building celebrated its third inauguration. Since then, Maison Curutchet has been well conserved, although its function is completely different from that for which it was conceived. The ground floor remains the area of traffic, while the vestibule serves as the reception area for the Colegio. The more public-oriented offices, which receive professional architects and the general public for a variety of legal procedures, are located in Dr. Curutchet's clinic. The residence volume has been reserved for the internal activities of the Colegio—the lower level for meeting and conference rooms; the upper level, for private offices. The interested visitor is allowed to tour the entire building without restrictions, and thus follow the journey through the promenade architecturale, and marvel at this magnificent example of Le Corbusier's architecture.

NOTES

1 Williams to Le Corbusier, 21 October 1948; Fondation Le Corbusier, Paris, Dossier Amancio Williams (FLC R3 07): 212.
2 Most likely Williams was not asked to become involved earlier in the process because his professional services to perform such tasks as site drawings would have been more costly than Curutchet's friend Ringuelet. The contract with Williams was understood to begin once the design had been completed.
3 Williams to Le Corbusier, 14 September 1949, Dossier Amancio Williams (FLC R3 07): 216.
4 Williams to Daneri, 4 October 1949, Dossier Correspondence Le Corbuiser (FLC EI 17): 182.
5 Williams to Prebisch, 1 October 1949, Dossier Correspondence Le Corbusier (FLC EI 17): 184.
6 Williams to Daneri, 4 October 1949, Dossier Correspondence Le Corbusier (FLC EI 17): 181-2.
7 Daneri to Williams, 7 October 1949, Dossier Correspondence Le Corbusier (FLC EI 17): 183.

8 Daneri to Williams, 22 October 1949, Dossier Correspondence Le Corbusier (FLC EI 17): 185.
9 Daneri to Williams, 17 November 1949, Dossier Correspondence Le Corbusier (FLC EI 17): 187.
10 "*Recibí el contrato. . . . En el tiempo en que encargué los planos a Le Corbusier, de mi casa, . . . yo tenía el dinero para la casa y un excedente de renta que unido a lo demás me completaban un presupuesto cómodo. Hoy todo el capital junto solo me alcanza para pagar media casa. . . . Por el momento desisto de la firma del contrato. Si la situación tarda demasiado en definirse, hasta encaro la sacrilega posibilidad de abandonar el hermoso projecto de Le Corbusier y hacer más adelante una casa de más fácil ejecución, que pueda hacerse en La Plata.*" Curutchet to Williams, 5 November 1949, Dossier Correspondence Le Corbusier (FLC EI 17): 186.
11 Williams to Curutchet, 12 November 1949, Dossier Correspondence Le Corbusier (FLC EI 17): 189.
12 Curutchet to Le Corbusier, 27 January 1952, Dossier Correspondence Le Corbusier (FLC EI 17): 214.
13 Curutchet lived in Lobería (370 mi south of Buenos Aires); his site and the governmental institutions involved in the process were in Buenos Aires and La Plata (60 mi southeast of Buenos Aires); Amancio Williams' office was in Buenos Aires, but he lived in Tigre (60 mi north of Buenos Aires); Petersen was in Buenos Aires, but his company was closed for two weeks for the holidays. Moreover, the administration of the Banco Hipotecario changed in January, presenting additional, unexpected, problems. From letter Williams to Curutchet, 3 March 1950, Dossier Correspondence Le Corbusier (FLC EI 17): 193-196.
14 Documents not available. Information inferred from a letter Williams to Curutchet, 3 March 1950, (FLC EI 17): 193-196 in which there are references to a letter Williams to Curutchet dated 6 February 1950, and another letter Curutchet to Williams dated 18 February 1950.
15 Curutchet to Le Corbusier, 27 January 1952, Dossier Correspondence Le Corbusier (FLC EI 17): 214. (Curutchet sent this letter to Le Corbusier long after the events had taken place.)
16 Williams to Curutchet, 3 March 1950, Dossier Correspondence Le Corbusier (FLC EI 17): 193-196.
17 "*Después de todo el esfuerzo hecho esta obra no puede abandonarse, ya se sabe que las dificultades son hoy gigantescas, pero la voluntad de los hombres es extraordinaria y vence todo lo que de ellos depende. Abandonar esta obra sería un suicidio, yo le pido encarecidamente Curutchet, que pongamos el hombro juntos. . . . No se olvide, Curutchet, que únicamente a través de una tenacidad extraordinaria se resuelven las cosas para el bien.*" Ibid., 196.
18 Curutchet to Williams, 11 March 1950, Dossier Correspondence Le Corbusier (FLC EI 17).
19 Ibid.
20 Williams to Curutchet, 13 March 1950, Dossier Correspondence Le Corbusier (FLC EI 17): 197.
21 Williams to Le Corbusier, 3 May 1950, Dossier Amancio Williams (FLC R3 07): 217.
22 Ibid.
23 Jorge Silvetti, conversation with the author, Harvard University Graduate School of Design, July, 1990.
24 Curutchet to Le Corbusier, 30 July 1951, Dossier Correspondence Le Corbusier (FLC EI 17): 201.
25 Curutchet to Williams, 24 February 1951. This letter is unavailable; information inferred from the letter Williams to Curutchet, 21 September 1951, Dossier Correspondence Le Corbuiser (FLC EI 17): 206.
26 Ibid., 207.
27 Curutchet to Le Corbusier, 30 July 1951, Dossier Correspondence Le Corbusier (FLC EI 17): 202.

28 Upon compiling Le Corbusier's *Oeuvre Complète* into a single volume, the editors wrote that Dr. Curutchet had wanted to furnish his house with Corbusian furniture, but unfortunately at that time it was not possible. Boesiger and Girsberger, *Le Corbusier 1910-65*, 82.

29 *Enduído apomizado* is a special finishing process using synthetic plaster, which is then glazed with pumice stone. This issue emphasized again the same controversy concerning the choice between a company from Buenos Aires and a local contractor. Williams wrote to Curutchet pleading his case: "*[T]here is a firm—Anderson—that does it very well, and I was discussing with them the possibility of doing it in a very small building like your house in La Plata. . . . [I]t is actually an industrial secret that only a few specialized companies know.*" Williams to Curutchet, 21 September 1951, Dossier Correspondence Le Corbusier (FLC EI 17): 206-207.

30 Ibid., 206.

31 Curutchet to Williams, 11 September 1951, Dossier Correspondence Le Corbusier (FLC EI 17): 209-210.

32 This, and the following two paragraphs from a letter Williams to Curutchet, 21 September 1951, Dossier Correspondence Le Corbusier (FLC EI 17): 208.

33 Curutchet to Le Corbusier, 27 January 1952, Dossier Correspondence Le Corbusier (FLC EI 17): 215.

34 Ungar was one of two directors of *Tecné, revista de Técnica, Arquitectura y Urbanismo*, an Argentinean journal created around the so-called Grupo Austral, which included Le Corbusier's name as advisor. The Grupo Austral was a group of Argentinean modern architects, among them Juan Kurchan, Antonio Bonet, Jorge Ferrari Hardoy, José Vivanco, Vicente Peluffo, Alberto Prebisch, Eduardo Sacriste, and Wladimiro Acosta.

35 Ungar to Le Corbusier, 12 March 1952, Dossier Correspondence Le Corbusier (FLC EI 17): 217.

36 Ungar to Le Corbusier, 10 July 1953, Dossier Correspondence Le Corbusier (FLC EI 17): 220.

37 Curutchet to Le Corbusier, 7 January 1957, Dossier Correspondence Le Corbusier (FLC EI 17): 227-232.

38 Ibid., and also, letter Curutchet to Silvetti, 16 June 1978, The Curutchet Collection.

39 Germaine Curatella-Manés to Le Corbusier, 14 December 1953, Dossier Correspondence Le Corbusier (FLC EI 17): 136.

40 This complaint was despite Dr. Curutchet's original request to Le Corbusier to obtain as much sunlight as possible, which he considered a challenge to the architect because of the characteristics of the site.

41 G. Curatella-Manés to Le Corbusier, 14 December 1953, Dossier Correspondence Le Corbusier (FLC EI 17): 137.

42 Curutchet to Le Corbusier, 7 January 1957, Dossier Correspondence Le Corbusier (FLC EI 17): 231. This young painter was Alfred Hli, "a talented painter, member of a group of modern artists." G. Curatella-Manés to Le Corbusier, 14 December 1953, Dossier Correspondence Le Corbusier (FLC EI 17): 137.

43 Le Corbusier to G. Curatella-Manés, 14 January 1954, Dossier Correspondence Le Corbusier (FLC EI 17): 139.

44 Most likely painting had already begun by the time Le Corbusier's specifications were received. Dr. Curutchet later wrote to Le Corbusier: "I deplore that the color of walls is not what you had indicated." Curutchet to Le Corbusier, 7 January 1957, Dossier Correspondence Le Corbusier (FLC EI 17): 227-232.

45 Le Corbusier to G. Curatella-Manés, 14 January 1954, Dossier Correspondence Le Corbusier

(FLC EI 17): 140.
46 Enio Iommi, born in Rosario in 1926, was a founding member of the Asociación Arte Concreto-Invención. He studied with his father, the artist Enio Girola, and later with the Italian sculptor Enrico Forni. In 1945 he produced his first abstract sculptures. From *Art d'Amerique Latine 1911-1968* (Paris: Centre Georges Pompidou, 1992).
47 Le Corbusier to G. Curatella-Manés, 14 January 1954, Dossier Correspondence Le Corbusier (FLC EI 17): 140.
48 Le Corbusier to Curutchet, 24 May 1949, The Curutchet Collection, fifth and sixth pages.
49 Ibid., sixth page. Le Corbusier proposed that it could be done "*au lait de chaux ou a tout autre procédé de cette nature.*"
50 Ibid.
51 Curutchet to Le Corbusier, 7 January 1957, Dossier Correspondence Le Corbusier (FLC EI 17): 227-232.
52 Dr. Curutchet attributed this modification to Simón Ungar, who followed Williams in the construction supervision of the house. (Casoy, "Entrevista," 8). However, the partition had already been omitted (either intentionally or not) in the construction drawings produced at Williams' office, a fact probably unnoticed by Dr. Curutchet.
53 Casoy, "Entrevista," 9.
54 Alcira del Carmen Curutchet de Goggi, (one of the Curutchet daughters) telephone conversation with the author, Buenos Aires, December 1990.
55 Ibid.
56 Ibid.
57 Jorge Silvetti, conversation with the author, Harvard University Graduate School of Design, July 1990.
58 "Casa Curutchet; La Fundación Christmann, artífice de la recuperación," El Cronista Comercial, Suplemento de Arquitectura y Construcción (Buenos Aires), 29 June 1988.
59 The Fundación Christmann was founded in 1949 by Dr. Federico E. Christmann, a local plastic surgeon of international renown, and a friend of Dr. Curutchet. In 1985, one year before the death of Dr. Christmann, the foundation's new directors—Dr. Federico Deschamps, José Luis Tesler, and Hector Deschamps (disciples of Christmann)—sought to reinvigorate the public role of this non-profit institution. The selection of Maison Curutchet as the site of their activities honored the pioneering work of the two renowned local surgeons, Christmann and Curutchet, as well as their professional friendship.
60 Julio Grossman, conversation with the author, Buenos Aires, January, 1991. The architects have photographic documentation of this alteration.

It is not useless, I repeat, to read constantly into one's own work. The consciousness of events is the springboard of progress.
—Le Corbusier, *Precisions: on the current state of architecture and city planning,* 134

CHAPTER IV

INSERTION INTO
LE CORBUSIER'S OEUVRE

Maison Curutchet is emblematic of Le Corbusier's architectural search in the years that followed World War II. This period of his work was characterized by an implementation of the "new discoveries" he had made during the war years, a renewed interest in the regional and the vernacular which he had begun to develop in the 1930s, and a reevaluation of the architectural principles that he had postulated in the 1920s. Maison Curutchet is in fact the first house in which Le Corbusier tested the crossbreeding of these three periods, and serves therefore as a perfect hinge point between his early and late works.

From the outside, Maison Curutchet appears a complex sequence of planes, punctual interventions, solid masses and carved voids. The façade is defined by a series of horizontal bands projected upon the frontal plane. Above, the differentiated horizontal bands of the brise-soleils and pan-de-verres of both the clinic and the residence emphasize the independence of the two volumes, yet the repetition of these forms creates compositional unity. Below, the horizontal band of the ground floor is clearly marked off from the rest of the composition, thus differentiating the ground level from other parts of the building. Set back into the shadows of the building above, it expresses the detachment of the building from the earth.

While the pan-de-verres and the brise-soleils clearly indicate the private nature of the building above ground, at ground level the separation of the public space of the city from the private domain of the house remains ambiguous. Although free access to the ground level is prohibited by a protective, black-painted, open-grid metallic fence, from a distance the fence appears to blend into the shadows of the volume behind. The concrete doorframe inserted into this fence is thus the only highly visible sign at ground level of the differentiation between public and private.

This doorframe and fence, combined with the other elements that compose the building's façade (brise-soleil, pan-de-verre, and baldaquin) consti-

MAISON CURUTCHET

FIG 53. The building at street level.

FIG 54. View of the ramp, pilotis, glazed vestibule, and the young poplar tree. Taken from the area immediately after passing through the building's entry door.

INSERTION

tute together a three-dimensional membrane that must be penetrated in order to enter the building. Upon crossing the threshold through the doorway, the occupant finds himself within the area of traffic, the liberated ground floor punctuated by the rhythm of the pilotis and the spatially overwhelming presence of the ramp and the poplar tree. Continuing through the building, echoes of previous and subsequent buildings designed by Le Corbusier reappear in front of the observer, demonstrating Maison Curutchet's position within Le Corbusier's architectural work, and also revealing the architect's continuous rereading of his own production. To fully understand the importance of this characteristic of Le Corbusier's modus operandi in the design of Maison Curutchet, and its projection in subsequent buildings and projects, it is imperative to appropriately consider the insertion—that is, the genealogy, sources and legacy—of this building within the architect's oeuvre.

The Genealogy of Maison Curutchet
Stanislaus von Moos has suggested that all of Le Corbusier's buildings and projects could be grouped or classified into two families, deriving from two of his own prototypical mass-housing units: the Maison Citrohan and the Maison Monol. The Citrohan prototype, first proposed in 1920, revised in 1922-24, and first built in Stuttgart in 1926, was a pure, abstract and cubic form, isolated and adaptable to its site condition. Conversely, the Maisons Monol (1919)—a series of small row houses with undulating roofs like Catalan vaults—suggested a closer relationship to the site and an earthy sensuality.[1] Maison Curutchet clearly belongs to the first; like Maison Cook and other buildings of the twenties, it is a cross-fertilization of the Dom-ino and the Citrohan schemes.

The Dom-ino scheme, first proposed in 1914, was based on a reinforced-concrete structural frame of horizontal slabs, supported by columns and connected by stairs. This structural concept, free of load-bearing walls, liberated the plan, which could now be partitioned by thin and light non-structural walls designed according to function rather than dictated by structural need. A related consequence of this system was the liberation of the façades, which, due to the absence of supporting walls, could now be organized according to the demands of interior spaces. Le Corbusier believed that the simplicity of this system naturally lent itself to mass production, and thus could assist in resolving the serious housing shortage at that time in European cities.

MAISON CURUTCHET

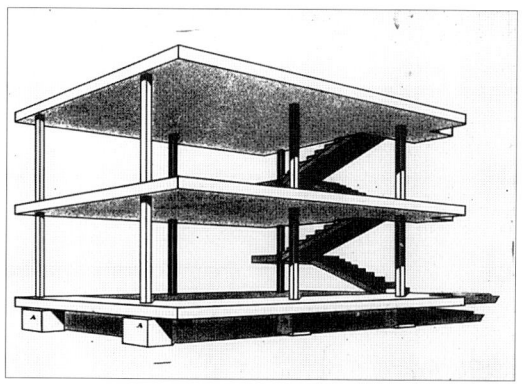

FIG 55. The Dom-ino structural scheme, 1914.

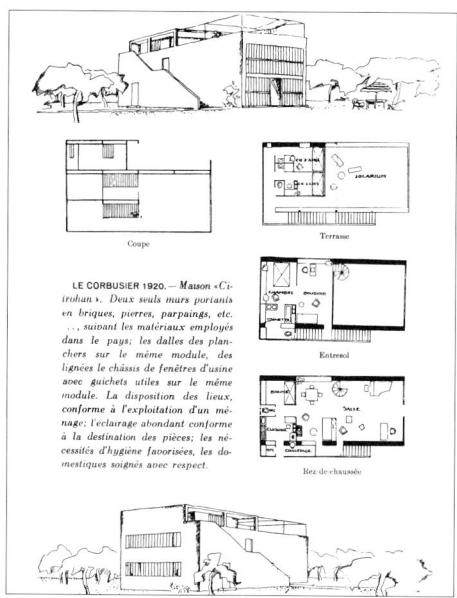

FIG 56. Maison Citrohan, 1920.

The Citrohan type represented the architect's sophisticated architectural interpretation of the typical Parisian artist's studio—an elongated, split-level space contained between two parallel structural walls. The interior was generously and naturally lit from a large two-story, fully glazed wall at one end. The sheer volumetric purity and simplicity of the Citrohan revealed Le Corbusier's preference for Platonic forms already praised in *Vers une Architecture*; as William Curtis has pointed out, the Citrohan type embodied the principles of Le Corbusier's "*machine à habiter*," a functional tool raised to the level of art.[2] These two schemes, Dom-ino and Citrohan, were based on the availability of new construction methods and materials, especially standardization and reinforced concrete. The synthesis of the two prototypes led the architect to one of his most famous postulates: the Five Points for a New Architecture (1926).[3]

The first complete and full-scale application of the Five Points was in the Maison Cook, built in 1926 in Boulogne-sur-Seine. This house is a synthesis of the ideas and principles advanced in both the Dom-ino and Citrohan schemes: an elevated cube, supported by pilotis, bounded by two lateral blank sides and offering large openings to the front and rear of the volume. The functional components of the house are contained in three stories suspended above the "liberated" ground level: the first floor houses bedrooms and private areas; the second, living spaces; and the third, a library and terrace-garden, the latter partially covered by a roof that gives the façade appropriate (square) proportions. The separation of vehicular and pedestrian circulation at the ground level corresponded to Le Corbusier's already formulated urban planning ideas. The nearly square plan is basically divided into four quadrants, defined by the structural system of pilotis, while the actual rooms are separated by thin walls that have no structural function. An ideal cubic container, it houses a carefully calculated sequence of compressing and expanding interior spaces.[4] While Maison Cook was the first full-scale achievement of Le Corbusier's synthesis of his own prototypical postulates for a new architecture, it also incorporated the purist and machine-age aesthetic, a search that he had begun in the late 1910s, and continued throughout the following decade until it reached its climax with the Villa Savoye in Poissy-sur-Seine (1929-1931).

The house for Dr. Curutchet was, as Maison Cook had been in the twenties, another blend of the Dom-ino and Citrohan schemes, and in fact shares many characteristics in common with the Maison Cook. The geometry of

MAISON CURUTCHET

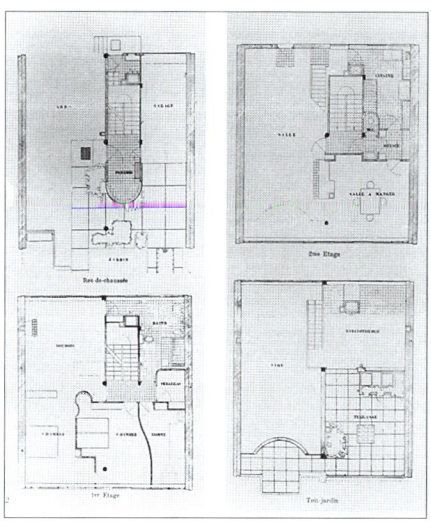

FIG 57. Maison Cook, Boulogne-sur-Seine, 1926. Floor plans.

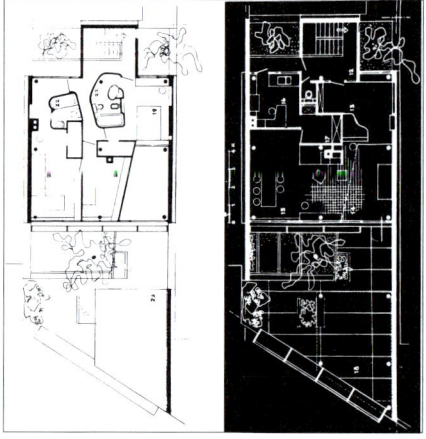

FIG 58. Maison Curutchet, floor plans of the residence.

INSERTION

the site, its proximity to the park (Maison Cook faces almost directly the Bois de Boulogne), and to some degree, the similarities of the programmatic requirements, posed an architectural problem that led the architect to reinterpret the solution he had adopted for Maison Cook.[5] The plan's organization into four quadrants, defined by the structural system of pilotis, is conceptually the same, including the more free organization of the bedroom level through a combination of diagonal and curvilinear partitions. Even the central positioning of the stairs, despite their obvious differences (in Cook they are placed within the cubical envelope, while in Curutchet they are attached to the rear side of the cube), and their related entry vestibules represent a reformulation of the same solution. Briefly stated, the design process and resolution of Maison Cook *informed* the design process of Maison Curutchet. It was as if the conceptual process of one project were prolonged and then inserted into the other, as if the two projects were one and the same. In other words, it almost appears that the creative process had been frozen in the subconscious of the architect for nearly a quarter of a century, awaiting suitable circumstances and the appropriate moment to finally be unleashed.

However, if Maison Cook is the Corbusian precedent to Maison Curutchet in terms of its volumetric similarity and resemblance in the organization of floor plans, the complexity and spatial articulation of Maison Curutchet's section recalls the first project for Villa Baizeau (1928). This villa, built in Carthage in 1929 (the built version is a revision of the 1928 project) is itself another variation of the crossbreeding between the Dom-ino scheme and the Citrohan type. In spite of their obvious differences, the longitudinal section of Maison Curutchet can indeed be read as a stretching, a displacing and a reaccommodation of the horizontal planes of Villa Baizeau's cross section (particularly the 1928 version; see FIGS 59 and 60). Furthermore, the "umbrella" roof that tops the building to protect it from the hot North African climate (the first Corbusian brise-soleil) anticipates the baldaquin of Maison Curutchet.

Influences from Le Corbusier's other previous projects and buildings may also be found in the resolution of Maison Curutchet's elevations. The street façade, which is slightly longer than the site's cross section because of the lot's angular relation to the street, is dominated by the clinic volume, which—bridging the entire front of the site—is clearly differentiated from the residential volume behind and above. These two aspects combined (the extra length of the site's front and the intention to volumetrically differentiate the

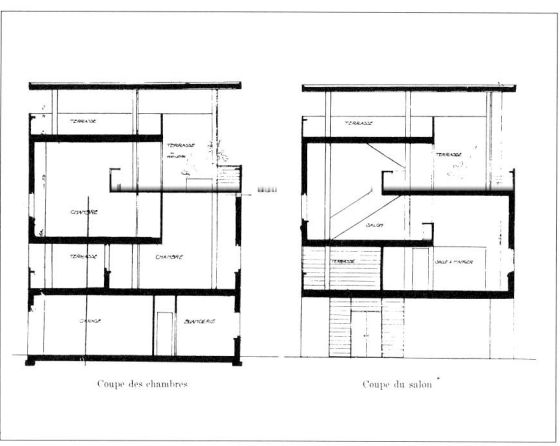

FIG 59. Villa Baizeau, Carthage, 1928. Sections of the first project.

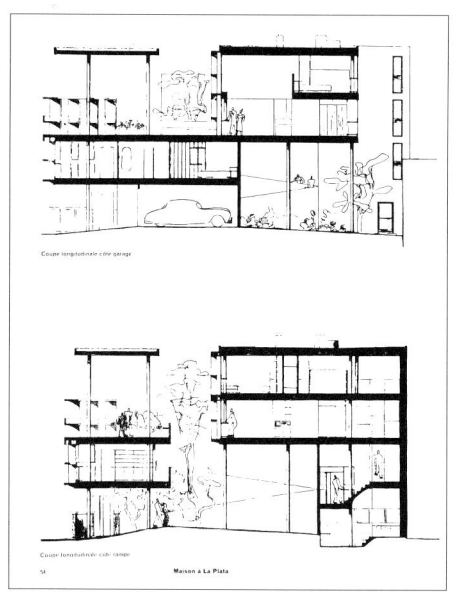

FIG 60. Maison Curutchet, longitudinal sections.

clinic from the residence), led to elevation studies resembling the street façade of Villa Planeix (1927), itself another variation, yet not as pure, of the Dom-ino and Citrohan types.[6]

Early studies for the resolution of Maison Curutchet's street façade, undertaken during the first few weeks of the project's development, confirm similarities with the solution adopted for Villa Planeix (FIG 61). Initially, the clinic was resolved with a three-bay structural system (as in Villa Planeix), in opposition to the dwelling's two-bay structure (as in Villa Cook). The three-bay structure of the frontal volume led to façade studies that resembled aspects of Villa Planeix, such as a symmetrical front, the projection of a volume emphasizing the entrance to the building (FIG 62), and an intensification of the stratification and succession of vertical planes parallel to the façade's plane. However, this line of investigation was partially abandoned after the critical revision of the project undertaken by Le Corbusier on March 9, 1949, when he established a two-bay structural system for the entire building.

Once the two-bay structural system was also imposed on the frontal volume of Maison Curutchet, the project again confronted compositional aspects already developed in Maison Cook. In effect, the resolution of Maison Curutchet's façade presents, despite its different vocabulary, strong conceptual similarities to Maison Cook's street elevation (FIGS 63 and 64). The ground floor is marked off as a dark horizontal band that emphasizes the detachment of the building from the ground, while the vertical plane above presents a carefully balanced composition. The cross-diagonal tension of Maison Curutchet's street façade, established between the entry doorframe and the baldaquin, and between the carved-out volumes of the garage and the unprotected portion of the terrace-garden, are conceptually similar to the diagonal compositional tension of Maison Cook's façade, between the semi-circular volume of the *parloir* and the protruding terrace balcony, and between the hollowed-out portion of the ground floor to the left and the cut-out of the façade's plane to the right. These diagonal tensions established between diverse components of the façade cut through the succession of stratified vertical layers that constitute it, exhibiting the phenomenological transparency that was typical of Le Corbusier's painting.[7]

The process of self-borrowing and constant rereading into his own work, however conscious as Le Corbusier claimed it to be, was far from a literal transposition of concepts or solutions from one project into another. Rather, he appropriated elements from his own production and reinserted them into

MAISON CURUTCHET

FIG 61. Villa Planeix, Paris, 1928. Façade.

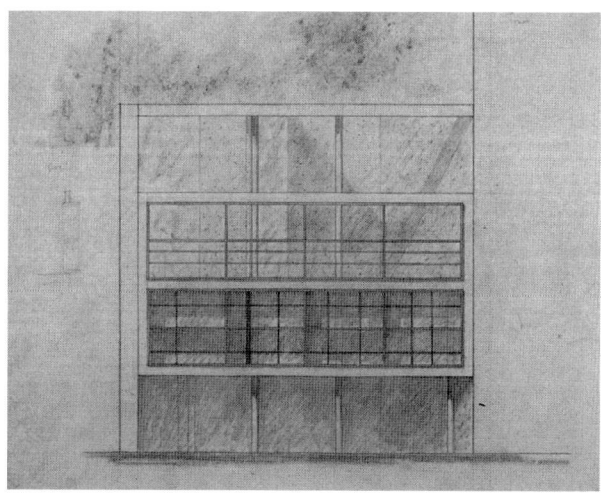

FIG 62. Early façade study of Maison Curutchet. (FLC 12161)

INSERTION

FIG 63. Maison Cook, Boulogne-sur-Seine, 1926. Façade.

FIG 64. Maison Curutchet, street façade at completion date.

new projects, demonstrating the endlessness of his architectural process and his constant search for architectural principles of universal application, which, nevertheless, he constantly reelaborated to confront the particularities presented by every project.

Maison Curutchet stands then as another member in the family of projects and buildings created from Le Corbusier's postulates for the modern house in particular, and for architecture in general. Nonetheless, the crossbreeding of the Dom-ino and Citrohan schemes, which originated as domestic typologies, was not limited to single-family houses (Cook, Baizeau, Curutchet, Shodhan). The Millowners Association (1954), located in Ahmedabad, India, and the Convent de La Tourette (1960), located in Eveux-sur-l'Arbresle, France, are variations on the same theme.[8]

Reassessment of Architectural Principles and New Discoveries
The projects, buildings and texts produced by Le Corbusier in the twenties had projected him as an architect of international reputation. In that period he formulated architectural and urban postulates of universal application for the "new" (modern) epoch. The buildings and projects he developed during those years represent a search that culminated with the design and construction of the Villa Savoye in Poissy (1929-1931). The following decade, the thirties, constituted a period opened to new investigations:

> The year 1929 meant to me, to a certain extent, the end of the first period of investigations. 1930 opened a period of new tasks; it relates to important works, great events in architecture and town construction, to the marvelous epoch of evolving a new machine civilization. . . . In the future I do not need to speak any more of a revolution in architecture, one that has already taken place.[9]

The houses that he designed in the 1930s demonstrate an interest in using a wider range of materials, especially those indigenous to the building's location, as well as an increasing concern in establishing a stronger formal interaction between the building and its natural environment. Maison Errazuris in Chile (project, 1930), Villa Mandrot in Le Pradet (1931), Maison aux Mathes in La Palmyre (1935) and the Maison de week-end in La Celle Saint-Cloud (1937), stand as the most significant examples of this new direction in Le Corbusier's domestic architecture. Despite this new direction, however, these works still absorbed and appropriated the modern spatiality that was

INSERTION

FIG 65. Villa Savoye, Poissy-sur-Seine, 1931. Exterior.

FIG 66. Maison aux Mathes, La Palmyre, 1935. Exterior.

characteristic of Le Corbusier's work of the two previous decades. World War II forced Le Corbusier to retreat from construction, and gave him the opportunity to further explore and define his new direction through intense and prolific writings. The most significant outcome of those years of investigation was the development and production of the Modulor.

When the war finally ended, he was able to incorporate his new discoveries with the principles he had developed in the 1920s, reassessing his previous concepts and blending them with the new in yet another, newer phase in his work. William Curtis rightly characterized this period: "1947 to 1954 was as fruitful as the 1920s had been, but the obsessive, forward looking utopia was now replaced by a mellow assessment of timeless values and an obsession with the harmony of nature."[10] It was a period during which his work exhibited a much more explicit concern with regional aspects of architecture, elaborating further on the vernacular concerns he had begun to develop before the war.[11] By blending together his architectural postulates of the twenties (the Five Points, the *machine à habiter* concept, the use of newly available materials and techniques, and his prototypical mass-housing schemes) with his new discoveries (especially the brise-soleil, the pan-de-verre and the Modulor) Le Corbusier sought to establish timeless values and principles of architecture, which were nevertheless subjected to local and temporal conditions. The most significant buildings and projects of this period—the Marseilles Unité, Ronchamp, Roq et Rob, and Maison Curutchet—are precursors of the sheer expressive monumentality of his later work.

In Maison Curutchet, the implementation of the Five Points is as pure and didactic as it had been in Maison Cook and in Villa Savoye, and in some cases even more so. The reinforced concrete pilotis provide the building with an independent structural system, detaching it from the damp soil and leaving the ground floor as an area exclusively dedicated to pedestrian and vehicular traffic, and to gardens. The roof of the clinic is regained as a terrace-garden, an enjoyable outdoor living space overlooking the park. The pilotis liberate the plan from structural walls, allowing thin partitions of varied geometrical configurations to define functional areas, and establish a frank counterpoint to the orthogonal structural grid and to the existing rectilinear boundary walls. The elongated window, which had been clearly identifiable in Maison Cook, Villa Stein-de Monzie and Villa Savoye, is in Maison Curutchet replaced by a full-height pan-de-verre (a direct consequence of the "discovery" of the brise-soleil). This partition in horizontal bands of alternately translucent and transparent planes fulfills the same objective as the *fenêtre à longueur*: to allow natural light to penetrate the entire width of the building. Finally, the façade, devoid of any structural function thanks to the setback position of the pilotis, is a light membrane that spans the full width of the site, as well as the full height of the volumes as determined by their respective floor slabs.

In addition to its clear position within the legacy of Le Corbusier's domestic architecture, Maison Curutchet also stands as a metaphor and a demonstration of the architect's urban ideas. Although much less dramatic than in the Villa Savoye and the Pavillion Suisse, and despite the site's constricted dimensions, Maison Curutchet is representative of Le Corbusier's use of a single building as a testing ground for his urban principles, particularly the differentiation between vehicular and pedestrian zones. The ground floor is completely dedicated to circulation, an area for walking, moving, and parking. Vehicular and pedestrian routes are clearly separated: the car enters on one side, while pedestrian circulation is on the other, its entrance appropriately emphasized by the framed doorway. The ground floor is also an area for vegetation, which grows through the vertical shafts to reach and "oxygenate" the upper levels of the building.

While Le Corbusier had previously explored these ideas—applying his urban concepts at the scale of a single house, and incorporating each of the Five Points—in his earlier domestic work, in Maison Curutchet he now reapplied these older concepts in combination with the newer directions he was experimenting with in his postwar design years. One such direction was his increasing attention to the context of the building's locale and site.[12] On his trip to South America in 1929, Le Corbusier had visited, among other cities, La Plata and Buenos Aires. Precisely in La Plata, where the Maison Curutchet would later be built, he first observed the *casa chorizo*, or "sausage house," a traditional local housing typology.[13] Probably without knowing its nickname, or that it is a direct descendant of the colonial *casa con patio* type, Le Corbusier was struck by the planning wisdom of this vernacular housing type and explained it with a sketch that appeared later in *Précisions*.[14] Like the abundant and anonymous casas chorizo it is surrounded by in Argentina, Maison Curutchet consists of a series of rooms organized around an open space through which the rooms receive natural light and ventilation, allowing the house to breathe. However, following his other, earlier postulates—most notably the need to detach living spaces from the damp earth—the architect

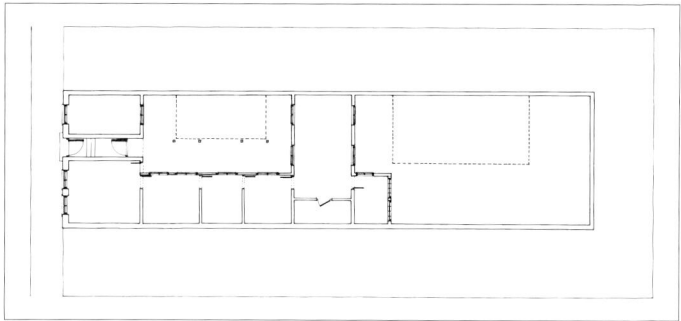

FIG 67. Plan of a typical *casa chorizo*.

FIG 68. Le Corbusier's sketch of the *casa chorizo*, after having seen this typology during his visit to La Plata in 1929.

eliminated the patio of the casa chorizo as an occupiable space, and transformed it into the void of the building's respiratory system (the hanging garden). Whether through an intentional or unintentional thought process, Maison Curutchet may be considered Le Corbusier's modern reinterpretation of the casa chorizo, a crossbreeding of his own architectural postulates with the typological characteristics of local domestic architecture.

Simultaneous with, and in spite of, his interest in regionalist aspects, Le Corbusier also continued his search to find and establish principles of universal application, most notably through the Modulor, his latest "invention." Thus, Maison Curutchet also became a testing laboratory at the scale of the single-family house for this proportional device, the most recent of Le Corbusier's inventions. The Modulor condensed Le Corbusier's earlier research and interests, including standardization and mass production, proportional systems, music and mathematics.[15] The building in La Plata is the first single-family house fully regulated by Modulor dimensions, from floor-to-ceiling heights, to minor details of equipment. In fact, as discussed earlier, Le Corbusier demanded special efforts from the client and his site architect to obtain authorization from local authorities to build the house according to Modulor dimensions. Once authorized, Williams tried to implement these dimensions as fully as possible throughout the building, despite the limitations of local industry and materials.

Maison Curutchet is also the first house, and one of the very first completed buildings, that features a brise-soleil as a sun-protection device for the fully glazed façade. This element later became a signature of Le Corbusier's postwar buildings, not unlike the pilotis and the nautical image had been in the twenties. Alan Colquhoun has brilliantly explained the role of this distinctive element in Le Corbusier's late work:

> The brise-soleil was a means of counteracting the vulnerability of the fully glazed façade to heat gain without having to return to the traditional hole-in-wall solid façade. In a manner wholly characteristic of Le Corbusier's dialectical logic, the ideal transparency of the external wall was not abandoned; its effects were counteracted by the addition of a new element. But the brise-soleil was more than a technical device; it introduced a new architectural element in the form of a thick, permeable wall, whose depth and subdivisions gave the façade the modeling and aedicular expression which had been lost with the suppression of the window and the pilasters.[16]

The brise-soleils of Maison Curutchet are concrete screens detached from the building's façades, similar in concept and design to its contemporary at the Duval factory in Saint Dié. The two nearly identical sets of brise-soleils at Maison Curutchet protect the northern, fully glazed façades of the clinic and the residence from sun exposure. Each consists of a system of vertical and horizontal concrete planes of equal thickness in all directions. In spite of their weight, these structures appear as light membranes floating in front of and independent from the pan-de-verres. By their position and orientation within the site, they are clearly depicted as two elements that belong to different volumetric units within the same container.

The first brise-soleil seems to float above the dark band of the ground floor, rising two stories above it. Its lower part protects the clinic's pan-de-verre, while the upper part acts both as a physical boundary to the edge of the terrace-garden, and as a device that frames views of the park. Moreover, by not extending to the ground floor, it acts as a visual "limit" that further emphasizes the contrast between the functions of the ground floor and the upper levels—the former reserved for traffic, the latter dedicated to living and working. The second brise-soleil, screening the residential volume, is located deeper into the site and perpendicular to the party walls (as opposed to the clinic's brise-soleil, which is parallel to the angled street front). It fulfills a similar function of sun protection.

However, as Colquhoun has indicated, protection from heat gain is not the exclusive role of the brise-soleils. Although originally conceived of as glare-handling devices, they also direct and frame views to specific points of the surrounding landscape, yielding a series of still images of the park. Their delicate proportions, designed according to Modulor dimensions, provide the house with an "honorific façade."[17] They act as "signs" that explain the architectural resolution of the building: more than any other element of the façade, the brise-soleils visually describe the essential components of the program. Their differing orientations powerfully explain and display the unique geometry of the angular site; their forms at once screen and disclose the differentiated activities that take place behind and below them; and their similarity in design visually unifies the whole composition. Moreover, their positioning in the site follows the lines of the adjacent buildings, which, along with the play of shade and shadows produced by their partitions, helps to blend the building into the fabric of the surrounding street façades. Thus, the brise soleils also contribute to the

INSERTION

FIG 69. Maison Curutchet, detail of brise-soleil.

FIG 70. Maison Curutchet, detail of façade.

FIG 71. Maison Curutchet in its urban context.

building's insertion into the city context, despite its unambiguously modern architectural language.

In short, Maison Curutchet is one of the most fully accomplished built testimonies of Le Corbusier's transitional period between the heroism and radical utopia of the twenties and the more monumental, explicit regionalism, and softened utopia of his mature work. It is also a remarkable living lecture of Le Corbusier's reassessment of the architectural postulates he had forwarded in the twenties, and their blending and adaptation to his new discoveries, interests, and "new tasks," which led him to produce a "timeless" architecture.

The legacy of Maison Curutchet
There is no doubt that Le Corbusier's oeuvre as a whole was, and still is today, extraordinarily influential to the work of both his contemporaries and to the generations that have followed. However, to assess the influence that one single piece of his overwhelming production exerted upon the history of architecture and the work of other architects is a very complex task. As a single building, the influence Maison Curutchet may have had on the work of other professionals is even more difficult to asses for various reasons. These include its relatively small size and scale, its location far from the traditional centers of architectural production, and its dearth of exposure in international publications. Moreover, since Maison Curutchet is already, in itself, a product of Le Corbusier's converging ideas and principles on architecture and urban planning, the particular influence that this building may have had may be hidden behind the overall influence of his oeuvre. Nevertheless, it is important to consider the influence that Maison Curutchet may have had on local architecture (in La Plata and Argentina), and in subsequent projects designed by Le Corbusier himself.

There is little doubt that the opportunity to see a building designed by Le Corbusier and experience it first-hand played an important role in the formation of a whole generation of local architects. This influence may, however, be blurred behind the overall influence that Le Corbusier's work has had beyond geographical borders. Nevertheless, the particular complexity of the program and the rather typical local characteristics of the site—a rectangle comprised of one open side (approximately ten meters, or thirty-three feet long) and three "blind" boundary walls—provided local architects with the opportunity to reinterpret in their own designs (whether consciously or unconsciously) the master's programmatic and volumetric resolution of Maison Curutchet.

One of the most interesting examples of this reinterpretation of Maison Curutchet is the Casa Pesci and CEPA offices (1978), located only a few blocks away. Designed by Pesci-Accattoli-Rossi-Reimondi, a team of architects from La Plata, it consists of a mixed program that houses Rubén Pesci's family residence and the headquarters of CEPA, a small publishing company dedicated to architecture and the environment, of which Pesci is the editorial head. The site is a rectangular plot enclosed by three boundary walls with one side facing a beautiful boulevard. Thus, both site and program presented obvious similarities to those of Maison Curutchet. Pesci's building consists of two independent volumes separated by an open shaft; the frontal volume is characterized by a largely perforated façade that not only respects the street-front alignment, but also provides a generous outdoor, semi-covered terrace. Although the two independent volumes do not necessarily articulate Le Corbusier's programmatic differentiation of one volume for each function, the conceptual scheme recalls immediately the Maison Curutchet.

There are in La Plata and in the suburbs of Buenos Aires many other houses and small buildings that articulate a similar volumetric solution to that of Maison Curutchet: a frontal volume suspended over a marked-off ground floor (often an open garage), and a rear volume housing other functional components, separated by a relatively large patio. But however similar in resolution these local projects may be to Maison Curutchet's scheme, the plasticity and poetic articulation of Le Corbusier's conception are absent to the point that it would be an exaggeration to consider these buildings to be modeled after Maison Curutchet. Rather, these houses may be regarded as modern reinterpretations of the casa chorizo, which, as previously mentioned, is a traditional and widespread urban dwelling type in Argentina.[18] Casa Pesci could thus be viewed as a product of both the legacy of the casa chorizo as well as Le Corbusier's own reinterpretation of this local typology in the Maison Curutchet.

While Maison Curutchet's influence may or may not be readily apparent in local architecture, its influence on Le Corbusier's later work is without question. His rereading of the casa chorizo type in Maison Curutchet was repeated in a conceptually similar strategy a few years later at La Tourette. There, he reinterpreted the traditional typology of the monastic complex, a series of wings and rooms around a courtyard, with a device that recalls Mai-

FIG 72. Casa Pesci, La Plata, 1978.

Above: FIG 73. La Tourette, Eveux-sur-l'Arbresle, 1957, aerial view.

At right: FIG 74. Maison Curutchet, aerial view of the model published in the *Oeuvre Complète*.

Lower left: FIG 75. Villa Shodhan, Ahmedabad, 1956.

Lower right: FIG 76. Maison Curutchet, street façade.

son Curutchet's resolution. Following monastic typological precedents, the convent's rooms and galleries are organized around an open space; however, Le Corbusier converted the traditional occupiable patio of the convent into a conceptual and sacred void. Therefore, and despite the obvious differences between the two buildings, the transformation of the casa chorizo's patio into a hollowed-out open space in Maison Curutchet, may be regarded as the immediate conceptual Corbusian precedent to the transformation of the monastic patio into La Tourette's central void. For an architect who had already affirmed in 1929 that it was not useless to reread his own work, this was far from coincidental; it was "the springboard of progress."

Maison Curutchet is also equally significant within Le Corbusier's oeuvre to aid understanding of the Villa Shodhan. This house, built in 1956 and located in Ahmedabad, India, is the last in the line of Corbusian houses which, starting with the Dom-ino scheme, passes through Villa Baizeau in Carthage (1928) and Maison Curutchet (1949). Although Villa Shodhan's site and its regional climatic characteristics are much closer to Villa Baizeau's resolution, the building owes much to Maison Curutchet.[19] The complexity of the section, the spatial interpretation of volumes contained within a conceptual box, the perforated façade dotted with brise-soleils, and the semi-covered outdoor spaces establish, indeed, a direct link to the house located in La Plata. As Jorge Silvetti noted, Maison Curutchet is certainly a turning point in Le Corbusier's design of houses, a landmark in the architect's work, and thus a landmark in the history of architecture.[20] Yet, its significance goes beyond these historic facts; its importance lies more in the intelligence and didactic nature of its resolution, and especially in the overwhelming spatial poetry that emanates from its architecture.

NOTES

1. von Moos, *Le Corbusier, Elements of a Synthesis*, 95.
2. Curtis, *Le Corbusier, Ideas and Forms*, 54.
3. The Five Points are the pilotis, the roof garden, the free plan, the elongated window and the free façade. For excellent discussions of the Five Points see for example: von Moos, *Le Corbusier, Elements of a Synthesis*, 69-74; Arjan Hebly, "The Five Points and Form," in *Raumplan versus Plan Libre, Loos and Le Corbusier*, Max Risselada, ed., (New York: Rizzoli, 1989), 47-54; and Werner Oeschlin, "Les Cinq Points d'une Nouvelle Architecture," in *Assemblage* 4, (October, 1987): 82-93.
4. Curtis, *Le Corbusier, Ideas and Forms*, 75.
5. This process of self-borrowing and self-reinterpretation was a typical and conscious characteristic of Le Corbusier's design process. However, despite the architect's acknowledged consciousness of this process, the similarities between the two projects were not explicitly mentioned during the design phase of Maison Curutchet. Aujame, conversation with the author, La Fondation Le Corbusier, Paris, 11 January 1993.
6. Like Maison Curutchet, the wider street façade of Villa Planeix is also composed of three bays, in contrast to the two-bay façade of Maison Cook.
7. For the phenomenal transparency of Le Corbusier's work see the excellent essay by Colin Rowe and Robert Slutzky, "Transparency, Literal and Phenomenal," in *The Mathematics of the Ideal Villa and other essays*, (Cambridge, MA: MIT Press, 1982), 159-183. For Le Corbusier and painting see von Moos, "Le Corbusier as Painter," in *Oppositions* 19-20, 87-107.
8. See Rowe, "La Tourette," in *Mathematics*, 185-203.
9. Le Corbusier, vol. 2 of the *Oeuvre Complète*, 3rd edition, (Zurich: Editions d'Architecture, Erlenbach-Zurich, 1946): 15.
10. Curtis, *Le Corbusier, Ideas and Forms*, 225.
11. The influence of regional characteristics had been suggested already in the previous decades. Paraphrasing James Stirling, the difference between Villa Baizeau and the Weissenhof version of the Citrohan is the exact difference between Carthage and Stuttgart. Stirling wrote: "Le Corbusier is actually the most regional of architects. The difference between the cities of Paris and Marseilles is precisely the difference between the Pavillion Suisse and the Unité." Stirling, "Garches to Jaoul: Le Corbusier as domestic architect in 1927 and 1953," in vol. 20 of *The Le Corbusier Archive*, ix.
12. In fact, within the first week of design work Le Corbusier requested his client to submit more detailed information about the characteristics of neighboring buildings and their site occupation. This point is elaborated upon earlier in Chapter 2.
13. The *casa chorizo*, or "sausage house," is a housing typology consisting of a series of rooms aligned one after the other (like a sausage) facing an interior patio. Typically the plot is bisected longitudinally into two equal halves, one half containing a series of aligned rooms, the other half, the patio. Often, additional rooms at the front and rear of the site enclose the patio, defining it as an outdoor space contained within the boundaries of the site.
14. Le Corbusier, *Precisions*, 228-229.
15. Curtis, *Le Corbusier, Ideas and Forms*, 164.
16. Alan Colquhoun, "The Significance of Le Corbusier," in vol. 1 of *The Le Corbusier Archive*, xlii.
17. Curtis, *Le Corbusier, Ideas and Forms*, 167.
18. The common modern reinterpretation alluded to would consist of a reelaboration of the interior

patio surrounded by rooms that define it. The frontal side, often aligned with the property line, provides an open ground floor as a garage that communicates to the open patio, yet does not drastically alter its spatial definition. All rooms are generally open to this patio space which, as in the casa chorizo type, is the heart and the most important means of natural ventilation and illumination of the house.

19 William Curtis has already noted that Villa Shodhan is a "suburban cousin" of Maison Curutchet and a direct descendent of Villa Baizeau. Curtis, *Le Corbusier, Ideas and Forms*, 210.
20 Silvetti to Curutchet, 15 May 1978, The Curutchet Collection.

What appeals to me is the magnificent phenomenon of architecture.... Architecture to me means construction achieved by a triumph of the intellect.
—Le Corbusier, *Oeuvre Complète,* vol. 1, 11

... but that which remains is established by the poets.
—Hölderlin, "Andenken"[1]

CHAPTER V

THE PROMENADE ARCHITECTURALE, THE EYE, AND THE POETRY OF ARCHITECTURE

Le Corbusier was fundamentally a poet. In opposition to his contemporary, functionally-driven architects, Le Corbusier was convinced of the need to elevate architecture from mere utilitarian construction to a poetic level.[2] It is precisely this elevated dimension of his architecture that distinguishes it from that of his contemporaries, and it is one aspect that projects his architectural legacy beyond the temporal and socio-cultural environment within which it was produced. The timeless poetry of his work remains today, thirty years after his death, one of the most substantial and provocative testimonies of twentieth-century architecture. The implications of Le Corbusier's poetics are manifold and encompass the body of his work, from the large-scale urban proposals to the smallest detail of an individual building.

Le Corbusier dedicated his life to pursuing poetry through architecture, an objective which clearly emerges from the abundant references to the sensitive and the poetic throughout his written work:

> For architecture is an undeniable event that surges in such an instant of creation that the spirit, preoccupied with assuring the firmness of a construction, of satisfying the exigencies of comfort, finds itself raised by a higher intention than that of simply serving and tends to manifest the poetic powers that animate us and give us joy.[3]

Terence Hawkes, a literary critic, has defined "poetics" as a concern not with content but with the process through which content is formulated; the "poet" is he who aims to disrupt stock responses, to restructure our ordinary perception of reality.[4] These two definitions, which Hawkes presents in a discussion dedicated to the literary text, provide an appropriate framework within which to analyze Le Corbusier's architectural poetics. Hawkes' definition implies that the poetic nature of a work (a text or a building) is not necessarily linked directly to its content, but rather to the orchestration of elements and the relationships established among those elements. That is, "poetry" is arrived at through the inflections of the language that formulates content.

This distinction lies at the very heart of Le Corbusier's architectural poetics, for it was through the language of architecture (a language that he contributed substantially to expand) that he pursued the disruption and restructuring of the ordinary perception of space, in order "to move men, move them through the effect of a thousand incidences which illumine the soul, surprise it, fill it to the brim, irritate it, rouse it."[5] His architectural vocabulary, that is, the elements he used to compose his buildings and projects and, above all, the relationship established between these elements, was the tool through which he constantly and systematically sought to affect the observer-occupant-participant's senses, to "irritate" and to raise them to a state of utter joy.

Le Corbusier expressed his poetry best through what he called the "*promenade architecturale*," that is, the calculated sequence of spaces and their relationship to one another. This was the medium through which his spatial poetry, the "thousand incidences," was incorporated into the cognitive and sensitive occupation of space. In fact, the development of the promenade architecturale is, perhaps, the singular, most important and non-prescriptive characteristic of Le Corbusier's architectural work. He explicitly acknowledged its importance for the first time in the text that describes Maison La Roche-Jeanneret (1923): "This second house, will be like an architectural promenade. One enters and the spectacle of architecture offers itself to the view; one follows an itinerary, and a great variety of perspectives develops."[6] This intentional tour-de-force was invariably organized as a carefully orchestrated sequential route through the building or group of buildings, leading to specific stations or "points of command" that offered visual and experiential interest. As Stanislaus von Moos correctly pointed out, the promenade architecturale represents Le Corbusier's intention to dramatize communication between the different components of a building or group of buildings.[7]

The promenade architecturale is intrinsically linked to the importance that Le Corbusier attributed to movement and visual perception—and particularly to the eye—in experiencing and occupying space.[8] Among Le Corbusier's abundant writings, the eye has always played a significant role, from the section entitled "Eyes that do not See" in *Vers une Architecture*, to the widespread consideration of visual aspects in *Le Modulor*. Precisely, in *Le Modulor*, the architect wrote: "Architecture is judged by eyes that see, by the head that turns, and the legs that walk"; and "I have stayed within the realm of concrete things, within the field of human psychophysiology. I have concerned myself only with objects falling under the jurisdiction of the eye."[9] The mechanics of physical movement, vision, and perception were paramount to his conception of the architectural "poetic moment." In *Le Modulor* he declared:

> And the poet that I am declares: in order to establish contact with the universe, man uses his eyes, which are at a distance of 1.60 meters from the ground. His eyes look forward. In order to look right or left he has to turn his head. His life, then is made up of a continuous sequence, succession, accumulation of visions. Man has a "material body"; he occupies space by the movement of his members.[10]

Movement and visual perception are thus the driving factors behind Le Corbusier's architectural poetry, clearly displayed in the unfolding of the promenade architecturale. This tour-de-force is generally organized as a sequence of circulation elements that lead to critical points of the building, which in turn offer aspects of particular interest: a framed view, a branching of the route, a place of arrival, command or contemplation. This sequential visual unfolding of space represents an act of occupation and possession of space through movement that resists fixation. Only the images appropriated and captured through touring the building may be fixed, however momentarily, and then stored in the mind, a strategy of perception similar to the sequential unfolding of images in a film.

In Maison Curutchet, Le Corbusier constructed an intellectual and sophisticated architectural discourse rooted in the visual arts and on the characteristics of modern times. He generated a sequence of architectural events, an invitation to discover the poetic dimension of his architecture. Not unlike those of the Villas La Roche and Savoye, the promenade architecturale of Maison Curutchet constitutes one of the most important architectural experiences of the entire building. It unfolds dramatically in front of the viewer's eyes through the careful orchestration of calculated focal points, perspectival adjustments, and framed views. From the exterior, the concrete doorframe marks the pedestrian entrance, the point of physical and visual penetration of the dense and complex interior of the building. This doorway is the focal point upon which the eye is directed, its actual form channeling the view toward it, further emphasizing it as the focal point. The framed door waits to be opened, an invitation to the progression of architectural events that lie beyond. It is not by coincidence that, when developing the building's exterior perspective, the vanishing point (the observer's eye) was placed precisely at this door, marking it not only as the entrance to the building, but more importantly, defining it as the starting point of the architectural promenade. Once the door is opened and the threshold crossed, the ramp dominates the visual field, attracting the viewer toward it, inciting the body of the occupant to ascend.

The ramp is undoubtedly the most important element of the ground floor, the main path of the promenade architecturale. As an isolated element, the ramp had always been a fundamental element in Le Corbusier's architecture, often associated with a poetics of movement through the building.[11] He considered the ramp capable of providing a completely different sensation than a stair: "the stairs separate floor levels, the ramp links them."[12] In Maison Curutchet, a transitional exterior/interior entry area occupies the space between the framed entry door and the ramp, establishing a tense spatial relationship between them. This relationship between doorway and ramp, and fundamentally the role of the latter in directing movement through the building, recalls immediately the Villa Savoye; further, the view from the midway landing of the ramp back to the entrance in both buildings is suggestively similar; however, beyond this point, the progression of architectural space in the two buildings is significantly different, yet charged with a similar poetic of movement.

In Maison Curutchet, the ramp starts at a spatially compressed point of departure under the volume of the clinic. Then, from the transitional space at the entrance to the upper levels, the ramp ascends gently, passing through a dramatic and varied sequence of semi-covered and uncovered exterior spaces, as it penetrates the parallel stratification of vertical planes, masses and voids (clinic, hanging garden, hollowed-out ground floor, brise-soleil, residence). Moving forward, the space compresses progressively under the volume of the residence above. Throughout, this sequence offers a variety of ambiguous exterior/interior vistas that evolve as the occupant advances through the ascending route. The ascending movement is interrupted half-way up the ramp at the midway landing, where the vestibule to the house provides an

POETRY

FIG 77. The concrete-framed entry door.

FIG 78. Preparatory drawing for the exterior perspective. Note the positioning of the vanishing point at the eye level of the doorway. (FLC 12162)

FIG 79. The open ground floor, circa 1954. The poplar tree that grew through the opening is not yet visible

FIG 80. View of the ramp from the intermediate landing, looking toward the clinic and the front of the site.

alternate route. At this point the promenade branches out, forcing the occupant to make a decision: to continue the ramp's path toward the clinic, or to access the vestibule to the residence, where the stairs will then take command of movement.

The adjustment of perspectival perception in the ramp's two ascending flights constitutes one of the most interesting and important characteristic of the building's promenade. From the point of departure at the ground floor, to the arrival point at the clinic level, the ramp negotiates 2.66 meters (approximately 8.75 feet); the intermediate landing divides the ramp into two parallel flights, each rising 1.33 meters (4.37 feet).[13] The slope of the two flights is basically the same, although the first flight is slightly longer than the second, which affects the angle minimally. However, the perspectival perception of space in each of the flights is radically different. The first flight, ascending toward the landing and the vestibule to the rear of the site, is markedly constricted by the taller parapet railing-wall on the left side, and the increased compression of the vertical dimension as the occupant progresses under the cubical volume of the residence above. Moreover, despite moving toward the landing area, which is bathed in natural light from the rear-eastern open shaft (also to the left), the occupant's eye is forced to shift to the right, focusing on the transparent box of the vestibule. The agglomeration and spatial succession of punctual elements, surfaces and masses on the sides and in front of the viewer's eye (tree, pilotis, garage wall, vestibule) foreshorten the perception of space, accelerating the feeling of movement toward the landing.

At the landing, the ramp turns 180 degrees to ascend back toward the clinic at the front of the site. The space becomes then perceptually wider, as light abounds throughout and views are multiplied. It is no longer a constricted space as in the first flight, despite the initially increasing compression of the vertical dimension; on the contrary, the expansiveness of the park invades the space at this mid-level, through the hollowed-out ground floor below and the succession and transparency of the pan-de-verres above. Glimpses and fragments of multiple framed views of the park catch the eye. Space is no longer foreshortened; rather, the view toward the park seems to expand the space beyond the building's physical boundaries, thus decelerating the visual progression through the ramp.[14] As the body moves forward, the spatial experience is liberating: the sky, the trees, the park, the pampas' expansive horizon, dominate the occupant's visual field.

FIG 81. Stair to the residence, seen through the vestibule's glazed front.

FIG 82. Villa Savoye's spiral stair.

As mentioned previously, the midway landing provides a branching point, a detour, in the promenade architecturale. Rather than ascending to the clinic via the ramp, at this point the occupant may instead access the house through the vestibule, which is dominated by the stairs' corkscrew configuration, an orthogonal variation of Villa Savoye's spiral stairs.[15] The ascending movement continues then up the stairs, which cut through the horizontal concrete slabs of the floors. Each level is accessible from landings that receive natural light from vertical, slit windows. These are covered by translucent glass panes, preventing any view of the outside from within the stairwell. Thus, the eyes search for a visual release, an expansion of the constricted space of the stairwell, a resolution to the tour-de-force. On both levels of the residence, this resolution is conceptually similar: after ascending through the constricted space of the stairs, the eye finds release in framed fragments of the wide park, which are presented only upon arrival at the landing. Whichever is the occupant's final destination, be it the lower level's living areas or the bedrooms on the upper level, the promenade culminates in privileged views of the park, which are captured in generous fragments through the frame of the brise-soleil. The views from both levels are at once different and the same: sky, trees, and the wide landscape of the park, which, projected and fixed upon the transparent surface of the pan-de-verres, invade the interior of the building.

The final resolution of the promenade architecturale is found in the terrace garden, which is located beyond the cubical container of the residence at the front of the site and is accessible from the living room. The terrace's baldaquin, conceptually an open tent, constitutes the end of the architectural tour-de-force. Under this baldaquin, a privileged and protected position for the occupant's body, the clinic's brise-soleil provides yet another version of framed panoramic views to the park. The occupant returns to the same vertical plane that was crossed in order to enter the building; however, the occupant is now displaced across this frontal plane and located diagonally from and above the point of origin of the promenade architecturale (the entrance door). After having participated in a magnificent sequence of architectural events, the occupant reaches this final destination, captivated by the building's façade. Here the occupant "becomes" a part of the "artist's canvas," upon which building and park merge into one.

The architectural, poetic experience that Le Corbusier had created and framed at Maison Curutchet was indeed the work of the artist. In fact,

FIG 83. View through the living room to the terrace beyond, from the area adjacent to the stairs.

FIG 84. Partial view of the terrace over the clinic roof.

POETRY

FIG 85. View to the park from the terrace, under the baldaquin.

painting had played such a fundamental role in Le Corbusier's conception of architecture, that he later claimed that the secret of his architectural quests could be found in his painting.[16] In his youth Le Corbusier had aspired to be a painter, and it was only because of the insistence and support of his early teacher, Charles L'Eplattenier, that he became an architect. Later, after he decided to settle in Paris in the mid-1910s, he met the painter Amédée Ozenfant who introduced him to the Parisian avant-garde and revived his desire to paint. Together, Ozenfant and Le Corbusier (then Charles Edouard Jeanneret) wrote *Après le Cubisme*, a book that not only served as the catalog to their joint exhibition at the Galerie Thomas in Paris, but also became an important art manifesto.[17] The text was a critique of the decorative excesses of cubism and proposed a revision of cubist postulates.[18] Whereas for Ozenfant purism was an exclusive *programme,* for Le Corbusier, it was only the first stage of an adventure that would branch out into different directions. In effect, not long after writing *Après le Cubisme,* Le Corbusier eventually recognized the importance of cubism; in later years he even liked to refer to himself as "a cubist."[19]

Nonetheless, purism became an important theoretical background, a springboard for Le Corbusier's understanding of architecture, as well as the development of his architectural language. His villas of the 1920s are a clear demonstration of the purist principles he implemented in architecture; these principles accompanied him for the rest of his career and may be uncovered in all of his buildings. Painting was a laboratory, a visual workout that the architect performed rigorously every morning; the rectangles, curves, proportions, spaces and colors of his paintings infused the plans, sections, façades and interiors of his buildings.[20] Painting was the activity through which Le Corbusier not only explored geometric and proportional systems, but also tested the precise relationships among compositional elements. The findings of this visual workout were then critically introduced in the development of his architectural projects, providing as well the raw material for the construction of an architectural discourse rooted in a visual poetics of space.

Le Corbusier's purist paintings were markedly non-perspectival; that is, they favored a single and unchanging vantage point. In them, mass-produced and mundane objects of everyday life (plates, bottles, vases, books, building components) were organized in flat layers parallel to the picture plane. The objects were shown straight-on, depicted in images that resembled their plan and section. The juxtaposition and vertical correspondence of their top and

FIG 86. Le Corbusier, *Nature morte à la pile d'assiette et au livre.* Oil on canvas, 1920.

frontal views reaffirmed that the viewpoint shifted only in the vertical dimension, a frank opposition to the cubist technique of encircling the object.

Maison Curutchet is indeed an outstanding example of the importance and effect that pictorial principles derived from purism had on Le Corbusier's architecture. To enter Maison Curutchet is, in effect, to penetrate the three-dimensional spatiality of a purist canvas.[22] In this regard, at Maison Curutchet there are three characteristics of purism that deserve special consideration:
- the layered sequence of vertical planes;
- the dissolution of the traditional foreground, middle-ground and background;
- the use of specific compositional strategies.

All of these qualities are clearly present in Maison Curutchet. The building is organized as a sequence of three-dimensional, parallel layers that are compressed upon the frontal façade (the picture plane). The entire lexicon of Le Corbusier's architectural language participates in intensifying this intentional vertical layering and slicing of space. The building's areas are arranged in vertical segments that succeed one in front of the other, front to back, in a clearly established spatial sequence: (1) clinic's brise-soleil and pan-de-verre; (2) ground-floor entry space, clinic rooms, and baldaquin; (3) hanging garden and terrace; (4) brise-soleil and pan-de-verre of the house; (5) living areas and double-height space; (6) kitchen, the upper-level bathrooms and master bedroom; and finally, (7) the stair tower with two open shafts flanking it. The ramp opposes this vertical stratification, cutting perpendicularly through it in an ascending movement that ties together and compresses these vertical slices of space.

Le Corbusier's clearly purist preference for a shifting vertical view point is, perhaps, most evident in his documentation of the project. The studies, perspectives and model photographs rarely show side views of the building. Rather, axonometric views, one-point perspectives and straight-on photographs predominate. For instance, in the publication of the project in the *Oeuvre Complète*, three model photographs depict the building from a nearly straight-on and identical point of observation that varies only in the vertical positioning of the lens of the camera. In the other published photographs, where the model is depicted diagonally from one side, the purpose is to show the open shafts through which the building "breathes."[23] However, Maison Curutchet also presented a special characteristic, because the irregular geome-

POETRY

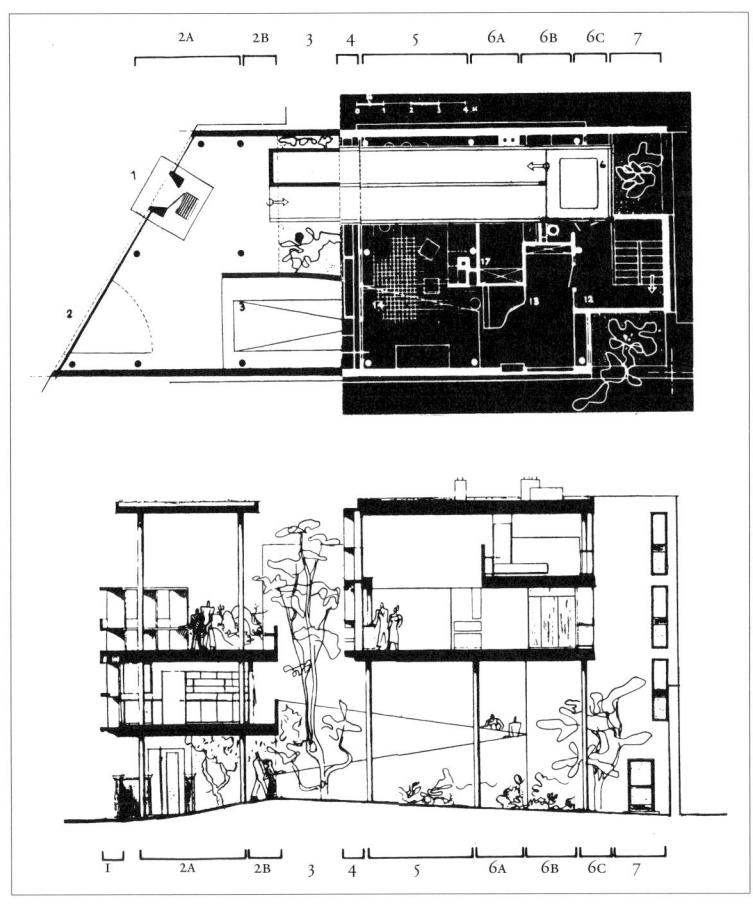

FIG 87. **Vertical layers in compression:**
Above, composite drawing of Maison Curutchet's floor plans; below, longitudinal section.
Numbers correspond to each section as described opposite.

try of the site's street front offered the possibility of a double frontal viewpoint: one, perpendicular to the site's front (preferred for perspectives and distant exterior views of the model), the other, related to the dominant geometry of the site, which determined the vertical layering of spaces and was the preferred viewpoint for studying the unfolding of the promenade architecturale as well as for close-up views.

Regarding the second purist characteristic mentioned above—the dissolution of the traditional foreground, middle ground, and background—Le Corbusier's purist paintings depict objects in vertical layers uniformly illuminated and tightly compressed upon the picture plane, an effect that tends to dissolve traditional pictorial organization. A similar principle appears in Maison Curutchet, particularly in the relationship between the two brise-soleils. The near-identical configuration of these two concrete grids, and their spatial juxtaposition, generates an apparent compression of one upon the other that defies the distance separating them. Moreover, the roof of the baldaquin lends a visual continuity to the concrete grid of the residence, projecting it farther into the frontal plane. This roof also drastically reduces the luminosity of the tall western boundary wall, which would otherwise have allowed one to read the actual distance between the two brise-soleils, and therefore establish two differentiated planes. Furthermore, the light that pours through the hanging garden backlights the elements (rooms, walls, pilotis) situated behind the frontal plane, perceptually pushing them toward the front. Thus, all elements receive a rather uniform light that telescopes the whole composition upon the frontal plane, and dissolves the three grounds; the entire building appears to be compressed upon a thin layer of space that challenges the dominant depth of the site.

The third technique that Le Corbusier borrowed from his purist paintings concerns compositional strategies in the building's design, particularly for the study of façades. From the beginning of his career Le Corbusier considered the façade as a plane to treat aesthetically like a two-dimensional canvas. In this regard, two aspects of Le Corbusier's purist paintings deserve special consideration: the predominance of a horizontal composition held in equilibrium by vertical elements, and the use of proportional and geometric systems that guaranteed beauty.[24] In Maison Curutchet, the two most important façade elements, the brise-soleils and the pan-de-verres, are predominantly horizontal, (even in their partitioning, horizontal elements are thicker and thus visually dominant). The overall composition depicts a sequence of vertically layered, horizontal bands: the carved-out ground floor, the brise-soleil of the clinic, and the brise-soleil of the house above. Not unlike a purist painting, this dominant horizontal composition is counter-pointed—"checked," in Robert Slutzky's words[25]—by two punctual vertical elements, the framed entryway and the terrace baldaquin. Both of these establish a conceptual symmetry in the composition, yet another purist characteristic.

Concerning the second point, Le Corbusier believed strongly that certain proportions and pure geometric shapes were indisputably more beautiful than others, and regularly used them to compose his paintings, sculptures and buildings. The façade of Maison Curutchet is determined by a system of regulating lines and proportional principles strongly related to the architect's compositional strategies in painting. The clinic's brise-soleil, for instance, offers an interesting case for study. In Le Modulor, where Le Corbusier presented at length his ideas and discoveries concerning proportional systems, he explained the composition of some of his paintings:

> [I]t will be seen that the lines do not begin at the four corners of the canvas but leave a free space on two sides. . . . The unforewarned art pundit may try without success to find in these paintings the trace of regulating lines starting at the four corners of the canvas; he will fail, or his conclusions will be contrived.[26]

Interestingly, the composition of the clinic's brise-soleil strictly follows the pictorial strategy described above: the concrete grid "floats" in front of the whole building, becoming a focal point within the façade's composition; furthermore, it is asymmetrically attached to the front wall, constituting a remarkable transposition and rare literal application of the compositional strategies originated in the painting laboratory.

Thus, by incorporating his compositional painting strategies, Le Corbusier was able to organize architectural elements in a spatial and formal dialectical relationship, creating a vibrant, poetic dialogue. In this dialectic play of elements he displayed the whole of his architectural vocabulary and his "inventions" to-date.[27] The interplay he established between the rectilinear edges of the building container and the curved partitions of the bathrooms in the upper level of the residence, is a prime example of this play of forms. Le Corbusier also consciously manipulated the perception of openness through a careful design of the ramp's spatial sequence and its related "architectural events." These are just two examples of "the thousand incidences which illumine the soul" found in Maison Curutchet. However, it is in the consideration of the composition as a whole, and in the resolution of the architectural problems posed by the project (Hawkes's process of formulation of the content) that the building (the content) may be fully appreciated as a phenomenon of poetry.

It is precisely the relationship between the building and its natural and urban surroundings, an aspect that had already concerned Le Corbusier in the 1920s and 1930s, that emerges as one of the most significant dialectic themes of Maison Curutchet. The expansiveness of the park penetrates the building through the "empty" ground floor and the open shafts, while these void spaces in return frame views to the park and interact with the geometric components of the building and its urban and natural setting. Furthermore, the architect carefully indicated the planting of trees which would rise through the open vertical spaces, an eruption of verdure that represents the extension of the park's landscape into the realm of the house. In fact, the tree that rises through the larger space in the hanging garden separating clinic from house, recalls the tree of the Pavillion de L'Esprit Nouveau at the Paris International Arts and Crafts Exhibition in 1925. Stanislaus von Moos characterized the tree at the Pavilion as one of Le Corbusier's "*objets à réaction poétique.*"[28] Likewise, at Maison Curutchet, the tree is appropriated as an architectural element, incorporating it as an intentional and carefully calculated poetic object. It is an element that exacerbates and exalts the relationship of the building to the park, bringing the park into the confines of the site or, better yet, conceptually placing the building inside the park.

The tree in Maison Curutchet constitutes thus an element that Le Corbusier incorporated into his architectural language and charged with poetic implications. Along with the other components of his architectural vocabulary, it is a fundamental constituent of the building's spatial and visual poetics. Without these poetically charged elements and the careful spatial and compositional equilibrium, the building might not have been much more than a satisfactory resolution of complex programmatic requirements. With these elements, Le Corbusier proposed a sensual spatial experience, completing an aesthetic, lyrical composition. These poetically charged elements are by no means whimsical or mere "lyrical" attachments. As he said, "the point of reference for all relations which have the power to move us are objects; by objects, I mean of course objects that work, or function."[29] Le Corbusier's poetry of elements and events provides the building with a

POETRY

FIG 88. Pavilion de L'Esprit Nouveau, Paris 1925. Exterior.

FIG 89. Maison Curutchet's respiratory system. Photograph taken through the central void space.

FIG 90. Ramp, tree, light and shadow, the poetry of space.

tangible sensibility. It served to improve the living standards, physical as well as sensitive, of the "new man."

In synthesis, from the boulevard, the spatial elements of Maison Curutchet are already perceived as a phenomenon of poetry, a symphony in space. The brise-soleils, the baldaquin, the concrete-framed entry door, the pilotis and the poplar tree, appear all at once, projected upon the frontal plane and poetically articulated in a carefully balanced composition that announces the magnificent spatial sequence awaiting inside. There, the ramp—the key to the promenade architecturale—links the sequence of vertical layers orchestrated in a succession of architectural moments. The elements of Le Corbusier's architecture—ramp, pilotis, brise-soleil, solid versus void, a tree searching for light and sky, and the park present in every corner of the house—fill the occupant's eyes with a "thousand incidences." It is poetry in space, the phenomenon of architecture.

NOTES

1. Johann Christian Frederich Hölderlin, "Andenken," quoted by Martin Heidegger in his lecture entitled "Hölderlin and the Essence of Poetry."
2. von Moos, *Le Corbusier, Elements of a Synthesis*, 52.
3. Le Corbusier, *Precisions*, 83.
4. Terence Hawkes, *Structuralism and Semiotics* (Berkeley: University of California Press, 1977), 158 (on poetics), and 62 (on the poet). Obviously, these definitions are rooted in structuralist thought, and they are not the only possible definitions of poetics and the poet. I have chosen Hawkes' definitions because they provide a broad framework within which to discuss Le Corbusier's architectural poetics, at least in relation to Maison Curutchet.
5. Le Corbusier, *The Modulor 2*.
6. Le Corbusier, vol 1 of the *Oeuvre Complète*, (Zurich: Editions Girsberger, 1943), 60. However, hints of the promenade architecturale can be found in earlier buildings such as Villa Schwob (La Chaux-de-Fonds, 1916) and Maison Ozenfant (Paris, 1917-22).
7. von Moos, *Le Corbusier, Elements of a Synthesis*, 85.
8. For a discussion of aspects related to Le Corbusier and the importance of the eye, see two essays by Lorens Holm, "Reading Through the Mirror: Brunelleschi, Lacan, Le Corbusier. The Invention of Perspective and the Post-Freudian Eye/I," in *Assemblage* 18, (August, 1992): 20-39, and "Le Corbusier and the construction of *Vers une Architecture*," in *Writing and the Architect*, proceedings of the 1991 ACSA Southeast Regional Conference (Charlotte: University of North Carolina School of Architecture, 1992), 116-127. I have enormously benefited from my friendship with Professor Holm whose writing and comments on this point have increased my knowledge and engaged my interest in this important aspect of Le Corbusier's work.
9. This and the previous quote taken from Le Corbusier, *The Modulor 1*, pp 73 and 184, respectively.
10. Le Corbusier, *The Modulor 2*, 19.
11. For example, the ramps at Maison La Roche-Jeanneret, Villa Savoye, the Carpenter Center for Visual Studies at Harvard University, and the Millowners Association in Ahmedabad.
12. Caption to the section on Villa Savoye, Le Corbusier, vol 2 of the *Oeuvre Complète*, 25.
13. The ramp started at +0.74 meters, the intermediate landing was at elevation point +2.07 meters, and the clinic level was at +3.40 meters; see drawing CUR 4111 "Coupe sur la ramp" (FLC 12115) from the set of drawings sent by Le Corbusier to Dr. Curutchet. *The Le Corbusier Archive*, volume 19, 240.
14. In the actual building, the second flight of the ramp is slightly less steep than the first due to minor dimensional adjustments in the construction phase, thus increasing this perception of spatial deceleration.
15. The image of the corkscrew, a penetrating element, is deeply related to the Dom-ino concept, in which independent reinforced concrete slabs are supported by pilotis and linked by an independent staircase that penetrates through the horizontal planes. Villa Savoye's spiral stair is the most remarkable and metaphorically clear example of this concept. It is important to recall that the project's original stair at Maison Curutchet was modified by Le Corbusier following a proposal forwarded by Amancio Williams.
16. Le Corbusier, *The Modulor 2*, 296.
17. Amédée Ozenfant and Charles Edouard Jeanneret, *Après le Cubisme* (Paris, Éditions des Commentaires, 1918).

18 For a treatment of purism see, for example, Robert Slutzky, "Après le Purisme," in *Assemblage* 4, 94-101; see also von Moos, *Le Corbusier, Elements of a Synthesis*, especially Chapter 2, "Purism," 37-56, and Curtis, *Le Corbusier, Ideas and Forms*, Chapter 4, "Paris, Purism and 'L'Esprit Nouveau,'" 48-57.
19 In *The Modulor* Le Corbusier wrote of himself: "Being a cubist, he had a bent for plastic phenomena, and his reasoning was visual." Le Corbusier, *The Modulor 1*, 29.
20 Curtis, *Le Corbusier, Ideas and Forms*, 50.
22 For a discussion of Le Corbusier's paintings see also, von Moos, "Le Corbusier as Painter," in *Oppositions* 19/20, 87-107.
23 See the publication of the project in Le Corbusier, *Oeuvre Complète 1946-1952*, 2nd edition, (Zurich: Editions Girsberger, 1955), 50-57.
24 The first of these two characteristics was noted by Slutzky in "Après le Purisme," 96; the second by Curtis in *Le Corbusier, Ideas and Forms*, 50.
25 See Slutzky, "Après le Purisme," 96.
26 Le Corbusier, *The Modulor 1*, 214
27 For a good essay on Le Corbusier as a dialectician, see Alan Plattus, "Le Corbusier: A Dialectical Itinerary," in Deborah Gans, *The Le Corbusier Guide* (New York: Princeton Architectural Press, 1987), 9-25.
28 von Moos, *Le Corbusier, Elements of a Synthesis*, 286.
29 As quoted by von Moos, Ibid., 307.

SOURCES OF ILLUSTRATIONS

All illustrations courtesy of La Fondation Le Corbusier in Paris, with the exception of the following. Numbers refer to corresponding figure numbers throughout the book.

9, 10	Archivos Amancio Williams, Buenos Aires
v, vi, 7, 47, 64, 79	The Curutchet Collection, Francis Loeb Library, Harvard University
8	Curutchet, Pedro D. From *Aximanual Surgery, Technology and History*
51, 52	Grossman, Luis and Julio
I, II, VII, VIII, 16, 53, 61, 65, 67, 69, 71, 72, 76, 80, 81, 82, 84, 85, 87, 89, 90	Lapunzina, Alejandro
39, 46, 77	Meszel, Claudio
11, 12	Municipalidad de La Plata, Argentina
4, 5	Otero, Néstor Julio; Photographed by Alejandro Leverato

BIBLIOGRAPHY

List of texts and other bibliographical sources directly related to Maison Curutchet and to the work of Le Corbusier:

SPECIAL COLLECTIONS:
Fondation Le Corbusier, Paris, France
   (correspondence, photographs, notes, drawings, books, articles)
   Dossier Aujame, Roger; (correspondence) FLC E1-4, xiv
   Dossier Curatella-Manés; (correspondence) FLC E1-17, 127-138
   Dossier Curutchet, Pedro; (correspondence) FLC E1-17, xxix
   Dossier Curutchet, villa du Dr.; (correspondence, drawings, notes, photographs) FLC I2-7 A, I to III
   Dossier Di Tella; (correspondence, booklets) FLC U2-13, ii and T2-13
   Dossier Ferrari; (correspondence) FLC E2-02, xi
   Dossier Martinez, Maison de Julián; (correspondence) FLC I1-17, iii
   Dossier Ocampo, Victoria; (correspondence) FLC E2-17, xxxii
   Dossier Plan de Buenos Aires; (correspondence) FLC T2-13
   Dossier Williams, Amancio; (correspondence) FLC R3-07, xv

The Curutchet Collection, Harvard University Graduate School of Design Frances Loeb Library Archives; Cambridge, Massachusetts (correspondence, photographs, slides, drawings from the Curutchet House)

BOOKS
BENTON, TIM. *The Villas of Le Corbusier 1920-1930.* New Haven and London: Yale University Press, 1987.
BOESIGER, WILLIAM AND HANS GIRSBERGER. *Le Corbusier 1910-1965.* New York and Washington: Frederick A. Praeger, 1967.

BIBLIOGRAPHY

Borthagaray, Juan Manuel, Jorge Glusberg, and Benoit Junot. *Le Corbusier y Buenos Aires*. Buenos Aires: Publicación del Cayc, 1981.
Brooks, G. Allen, ed. *The Le Corbusier Archives*. 32 vols. London and Paris: Garland Publishing and La Fondation Le Corbusier, 1983-86.
Curtis, William. *Le Corbusier: Ideas and Forms*. New York: Rizzoli, 1986.
Frampton, Kenneth, ed. *Oppositions* 15/16 and 19/20 (special double-issues on Le Corbusier). New York: The Institute for Architecture and Urban Studies, 1978 and 1980.
Le Corbusier. *Creation is a Patient Search*. New York: Praeger, 1960.
———. *The Modulor 1 and 2*. Cambridge: Harvard University Press, 1980.
———. *Precisions: on the present state of architecture and city planning*. Translated from the French by Edith Schreiber Aujame. Cambridge and London: The MIT Press, 1991.
———. *Oeuvre Complète*, vol. 1, 1920-1929. 3rd ed. Zurich: Editions Girsberger, 1943.
———. *Oeuvre Complète*, vol. 2, 1929-1934. 3rd ed. Zurich: Editions Girsberger, 1946.
———. *Oeuvre Complète*, vol. 3, 1934-1938. 2nd ed. Zurich: Editions Girsberger, 1945.
———. *Oeuvre Complète*, vol. 4, 1938-1946. Zurich: Editions d'Architecture, 1946.
———. *Oeuvre Complète*, vol. 5, 1946-1952. 2nd ed. Zurich: Editions Girsberger, 1955.
———. *Towards a New Architecture*. Translated from the 13th French edition of *Vers Une Architecture* (1927). New York: Dover, 1978.
Ozenfant, Amédée and Charles-Edouard Jeanneret. *Après le Cubisme*. Paris: Éditions des Commentaires, 1918.
———. *La Peinture Moderne*. Paris: Editions Frèal, 1925.
Risselada, Max, ed. *Raumplan versus Plan Libre: Adolf Loos and Le Corbusier*. New York: Rizzoli, 1988.
Rowe, Colin. *The Mathematics of the Ideal Villa and Other Essays*. Cambridge, MA: The MIT Press, 1976.
Russell-Hitchcock, Henry. *Latin American Architecture since 1945*. New York: The Museum of Modern Art, 1955.
von Moos, Stanislaus. *Le Corbusier, Elements of a Synthesis*. Cambridge: The MIT Press, 1985 (fifth printing).

ARTICLES AND ESSAYS

Asencio, Miguel. "Homenaje a Le Corbusier." *Nuestra Arquitectura* (September 1965): 15-22. Buenos Aires: Editorial Contémpora.
Aujame, Roger. "Maison du Dr. Curutchet à La Plata, 1949." *Techniques et Architecture* 373 (September 1987): 52-55. Paris: Editions Regirex-France.
Casoy, Daniel. "Le Corbusier en La Plata: entrevista con el Dr. Curutchet." *Arquitecturas Bis* 43 (March 1983): 2-10.

COLQUHOUN, ALAN. "The significance of Le Corbusier." In vol. 1 of *The Le Corbusier Archive*, xxv-xliv. London and Paris: Garland Publishing and La Fondation Le Corbusier, 1983.

DUPRAT, ANDRÉS. "Le Corbusier australe: casa Curutchet a La Plata." *Casabella* 573 (November 1990): 24-26. Milano: Elemond Periodici.

HELBY, ARJAN. "The Five Points and Form." In Max Risselada, ed. *Raumplan versus Plan Libre, Loos and Le Corbusier*, 47-54. New York: Rizzoli, 1989.

HOLM, LORENS. "Reading Through the Mirror: Brunelleschi, Lacan, Le Corbusier. The Invention of Perspective and the Post-Freudian Eye/I." *Assemblage* 18 (August 1992): 20-39.

———. "Le Corbusier and the Construction of *Vers une Architecture*, Towards a Metaphor Architecture." Proceedings of the 1991 ACSA Southeast Regional Conference "Writing and the Architect," Charlotte, North Carolina, 1992, 116-127.

LIERNUR, PANCHO AND PABLO PSCHEPIURCA. "Precisiones sobre los proyectos de Le Corbusier en la Argentina 1929/1949." *Summa* 243 (November 1987): 40-55. Buenos Aires: Ediciones Summa.

OECHSLIN, WERNER. "Les Cinq Points d'une Architecture Nouvelle." *Assemblage* 4 (October 1987): 83-93.

PESCI, RUBÉN. "Le Corbusier en la Argentina." *a/mbiente* 21 (August 1980): 61-68. La Plata, Argentina: Editorial CEPA.

PLATTUS, ALAN. "Le Corbusier: A Dialectical Itinerary." In Deborah Gans. *The Le Corbusier Guide*, 9-25. Princeton: Princeton Architectural Press, 1987.

SLUTZKY, ROBERT. "Après le Purisme." *Assemblage* 4 (October 1987); 95-101.

SOLIS, VICTORIA. "Nueva Vida y Función para una casa insigne." *Clarín*, Suplemento Arquitectura, Friday June 24, 1988. Buenos Aires.

SOLTAN, JERZY. "Working with Le Corbusier." In vol. 17 of *The Le Corbusier Archive*, ix-xxiv. London and Paris: Garland Publishing and La Fondation Le Corbusier, 1983.

STIRLING, JAMES. "Garches to Jaoul: Le Corbusier as domestic architect in 1927 and 1952." In vol. 20 of *The Le Corbusier Archive*, ix-xxi. London and Paris: Garland Publishing and La Fondation Le Corbusier, 1983.

VON MOOS, STANISLAUS. "Le Corbusier as Painter." In Kenneth Frampton, ed., *Oppositions* 19/20, 87-107. New York: The Institue for Architecture and Urban Studies, 1978 and 1980.

WARREN, JAMES. "Preservation, Corb in Context." *Progressive Architecture*, April 1989.

Other bibliographic sources mentioned in the text:

BOOKS

AYERZA DEL CASTILLO, LAURA AND ODILE FELGINE. *Victoria Ocampo.* Paris: Editorial Criterion, 1991.

CURUTCHET, PEDRO D. *Aximanual Surgery: technology and history.* Buenos Aires, 1974.

———. *Axitechnical Surgery and Crucimanual History.* Buenos Aires, 1976.

HAWKES, TERENCE. *Structuralism and Semiotics.* Berkeley, CA: University of California Press, 1977.

OTERO, NÉSTOR JULIO, ed. *Casas 25: Ocampo, Bustillo, Le Corbusier, Mendelsohn, Gropius, Prebisch.* Buenos Aires: Librería CP 67, 1992.

SILVETTI, JORGE, ed. *Amancio Williams.* New York: Rizzoli, 1987.

ARTICLES AND ESSAYS

BENOIT, PEDRO. "Descripción de la Traza." *a/mbiente* 32 (June 1982): 30-31. La Plata, Argentina: Publicaciones CEPA/ Espacio Editora.

KATZENSTEIN, ERNESTO. "Argentine Architecture in the thirties." *DAPA, Journal of Decorative Arts* (1992): 54-57. New York.

LE CORBUSIER. "Amancio Williams." *L'Homme et l'Architecture* 15-16 (1947). Paris.

RIGOLI, GIANNI. "The work of Amancio Williams." *Zodiac* 16 (1966): 37-68. Milano.